A WAY WITH WORDS

Words in Color in the Classroom Series

A WAY WITH WORDS

A log of ideas for creative writing in the classroom

EDNA GILBERT

EDUCATIONAL EXPLORERS

READING

First published in Great Britain 1968
by Educational Explorers Ltd
40 Silver Street, Reading, Berkshire
© Edna Gilbert 1968
SBN: 85225 533 0

Printed in Great Britain
by Lamport Gilbert Printers Ltd
Reading, Berkshire
Set in Monotype Baskerville

CONTENTS

ILLUSTRATIONS

To

TERRY *and* KIM
*who graciously ate their
dinner by the fireplace the many
times the typewriter usurped the kitchen table*

FOREWORD

I ONCE MET an American publisher to discuss a project I had been able to carry out in Britain. He was favorably inclined toward it since the English series was attractive and its concept compelling; however, he declined to undertake an extension of the series to include writers from the United States because in his experience Americans did not in general know how to write—very few cultivated writing, and the series needed people with a story to tell but who had perhaps never published a line.

When the typescript of this book reached my desk I read it at one sitting, so enthralling was its content and variety. I had never really accepted the publisher's view of his countrymen. Now I had proof that there is nothing preventing Americans from using their pen as other cultivated people do. For here was a writer, a teacher, and several other writers from her class of sixth graders, who had produced a document that excited and encouraged.

That the author should have found inspiration at a workshop at *Schools for the Future* was very gratifying and I am honored to have had any connection with this work. But I do not delude myself; the truth is simply that everybody, when properly challenged, can delight in becoming as expert as he can with a pen. Mrs Edna Gilbert found for herself a means of making her students become aware of their powers and talents, and that to write well and purposefully is a joy.

This book shows that ordinary students of all grades can be educated to take responsibility for their written speech, as they accepted responsibility for their spoken speech in communicating with their peers.

We write first for ourselves, to extend our capabilities, to meet challenges such as transmuting feeling into words. In so doing we experience a reward beyond mere acquisition of a skill; we become aware of deeper layers on the self and what happens there. Working on speech is one of the most exciting occupations man could find.

To communicate is important but it is secondary when compared with the meeting of one's creativity—the awareness, arising from total involvement in some subtle task, of what one can do with oneself and what one's culture offers.

I hope that my deep interest in this work will be shared by the teachers of English who see an opening for themselves in running classes of this kind.

It only need be added that the spelling and idiom of the original script have been retained throughout the book. This is to enable readers both in the United States and elsewhere to appreciate more fully the particular qualities of an American school environment, so openly recorded here for us.

Schools for the Future C. GATTEGNO
New York City February 1968

Chapter One

RESTRICTIVE SENTENCES

WITH INSPIRATION from a well-known educator and guidance from a sixth grade class, I discovered that creative writing could be an enjoyment that was considered a treat in a class-room situation. What a thrill to hear shouts of joy rather than groans when suggesting a writing assignment! Why such a change in attitude? It all started after a workshop in creative writing conducted by Dr Caleb Gattegno, well known for his creation of *Words in Color* (a new approach to the teaching of reading) and for distinguished contributions in many other fields of education.

Dr Gattegno, who for many years had been a classroom teacher, a professor at institutes of higher education in Europe and a lecturer in many parts of the world and in the United States, established a research center in New York (*Schools for the Future*) where he and his associates investigate more fruitful ways of instilling inspiration in the education of children. In the field of creative writing and in other areas of the curriculum Dr Gattegno advocated that activities be centered around the real gifts of each learner rather than any pre-conceived lesson plan prescribed by a text or prepared by the teacher.

Without any definite ideas on creative writing, our workshop group learned to work together with challenging word games which seemed to develop our own sensitivities and make us more aware of the problems and tasks involved in a writing assignment.

Following exposure to the reforms suggested by this inspiring educator, I returned to my class in Arizona with renewed energy and enthusiasm, but still dubious as to the lasting success of these new methods. Doubts first arose because of the use of word exercises which we called 'restrictive games'.

9

In these exercises children were instructed to write sentences within the confines of certain restrictions. An illustration of such restriction is found in a game involving the writing of a sentence using no more than three-letter words. The following are representative of sentences inspired by these rules:

A fly has his eye on my pie.

I saw a big red fox run to the top of the pen and eat an old red hen.

A big dog bit the boy on his leg.

This new approach stimulated interest and eventually students began to create new games for themselves. Some games restricted all words in the sentence to the same number of letters:

White paste dries clear.

Space study might boost Glen's grade.

Candy could taste awful.

Word games became a regular part of our language and as time went on our rules became more varied, causing a greater probing of word repertoire. I was amazed to see what could be produced using words constructed of only the consonants *m*, *s*, *t* and *r* with any of the vowels.

Sometimes I am tired.

At times Sue eats meat.

It is to reassure Tim.

Mister Moore sat to rest.

I had always assumed that creativity was best nurtured in a permissive atmosphere where freedom exists. 'Was not a restrictive sentence a loss of freedom of expression?' I asked myself.

To my amazement I discovered that students were being much more imaginative in their verbal expressions when given these challenges than when writing with complete freedom. The capacity to be puzzled seemed to immerse each writer deeper into the task at hand. The word games forced them to think; they were encouraged to manipulate language in order to follow the rules of an exercise.

Writing a sentence using nothing but words starting with the letter *s* or *m* or *p* would bring on such intense thought that one could almost hear the words being tested in each rapidly functioning mind.

Patrolmen patiently patrolled Parliament.

Pilgrims practised piety.

Papa puffs perfumed pipes.

Poverty persecutes people.

I was beginning to see that putting the students under certain conditions was fertilising the seeds of thought. These restrictions did not stunt creativity but on the contrary nourished it. They seemed to be a means of channeling thoughts towards a certain gain. With choices broken into smaller units greater efficiency seemed to arise. This approach might be compared to a child in a huge department store trying to pick out a new outfit. The task might take all day under normal conditions; but if he were advised to purchase a washable outfit to match a certain blue tie, his minimised selection would direct his thinking to a certain area of the store and still give him plenty of room for individual investigation.

How proud a child could be when he had accomplished a task such as writing a sentence using words of at least eight letters!

Enormous elephants stampeded Sacramento yesterday.

Bloodthirsty bloodhounds blockaded Frankenstein's laboratory.

Rebellious ranchmen revolted throughout southeastern territories.

Treasured keepsakes enriched Grandmother's memories.

After succeeding in this exercise one student said, 'I didn't know I could use such grown-up words'.

The enthusiasm was becoming infectious as we shared the

work with one another, and sharing was a great part of the enjoyment following the deep thought.

Realising that a first step in the creative climate was to help each individual recognise the importance of his own personal experience, I was careful never to scar a child by negative criticism of his accomplishments. Alex Osborn had the right idea when he said, 'Creativity is so delicate a flower that praise tends to make it bloom while discouragement oftens nips it in the bud'. And who is qualified to judge a child's creative efforts?

Since creativity is such a personal thing (what is unique and creative for one child may not be new and creative for another) I considered it my duty as a teacher not to evaluate but to shield each child from those things which might interfere with his productivity so that his careful probing would result in more fruitful outpourings.

In our first sharing periods the more confident girls and boys would volunteer to read their papers, but as soon as it was realised that everyone was safe from external evaluation each student was enthusiastic about sharing what he had written. With confidences strengthened, students attempted unique expressions, for they began writing for their own satisfaction rather than that of their teacher or class.

Not every effort proved to be a gem, but through sharing and writing children were able to gain in the process of choosing as well as the process of producing. They became their own critics. Through these actions renewed interests and motivations were built, and without threat of censure or guilt for experimenting with new forms of expression, our flowers were beginning to bloom.

Variety was being maximised as new games were being played. Words became a magic medium as children saw them transmit so many different messages. A game of working with word relationships and combinations proved the possibilities of power in the manipulation of vocabulary.

A given group of words to combine in a sentence brought forth such varied responses that one soon realised that the power was in the word relationship which each individual created. When the words *smelling, carrots* and *accidental* were given to a class of twenty-seven sixth graders, twenty-seven different results were obtained.

In an *accidental* fall the rabbit discovered a patch of good *smelling carrots*.

The *smelling* salts did not help the fat old lady since her *accidental* fall was caused by eating spiked *carrots*.

Because of an *accidental* mishap at the laboratory farm, green *carrots smelling* like onions were produced.

For a more rhythmical game the words *short, shade, sharp* and *shake* were given.

That *short* girl sitting in the *shade* is so *sharp* that she won a strawberry *shake* from our teacher.

Sit in the *shade* and watch the *sharp* shark *shake* his *short* snout.

Sharp tongued women can *shake* up more rumors as they mingle in the *shade* of the *short* alleyway.

He could not wiggle and *shake* as the musicians played the *sharp* teenage music because his hair was a *shade* too *short*.

It was evident to me that these writing games were bases from which strength in the communicative arts was developing. Another satisfying result was the way unknown aptitudes and powers were being released among my slower learners.

Motivation was high and we were ready to move on to more extensive challenges in creative writing.

Chapter Two

EXTENDED WRITINGS

THE GREAT VICTORIES in fashioning sentences from the restrictive field aroused such an eager response that children were anxious to extend their writings. With motivation at such a peak I knew that new meaningful exercises would bring forth more fresh, colorful innovations. As a result I was anxious to plan meaningful assignments which would allow the students to experiment with the manipulation of language to see what kinds of effects could be achieved.

With an eager group of individuals capable of wondering, we had one of the most important ingredients for creating, but now we had another need: a problem. As stated by Erich Fromm, 'Conditions of a creative attitude, of being sensitive, requires capacity to be puzzled'. Children seem still to have this capacity to be puzzled whereas many adults appear to lose their spirit of wondering, feeling they should know everything.

Early situations in paragraph writing were merely extensions of the restrictive sentences. Since each child had experienced the reorganisation of words into a complete thought, I asked them to do the same with a new group of words, only this time to write a story rather than a sentence. To further their puzzlement I suggested that their stories be completed in ten sentences with the first sentence beginning with the letter *a*, the second with the letter *b* and so on until they reached the letter *j*.

The words given were *whistle, eyelids, lightning, exhibit* and *straight*.

A *whistle* of wind rushed by. Big thrashes of *lightning* struck the town. Calmly I walked over to the window. Dust clouds seemed to be moving in a *straight* line.

Easily I opened the window and my hair blew back. Flying in were bits of dust. Gradually I closed my *eyelids* and tried to go back to sleep. Hopping up suddenly because of a loud noise caused by the wind that had blown my *exhibit* of horses to the floor, I was startled. I rushed hastily back to bed and pulled the covers over my head. Just in time, for just then Mother came in to see what had happened.

A big *whistle* came and a flash of *lightning* struck the house next door. Big flames burst out on the roof. Cindy closed and then opened her *eyelids*, realising she must call the fireman. Down the road came the fire truck in a matter of minutes. Excitement was everywhere. From the fire chief came many prompt orders.

'Get that hose hooked up,' he yelled, and an *exhibit* of efficiency was seen by the crowd.

Herman, Cindy's father, drove up. Immediately he jumped out of the car and headed *straight* for Cindy's room to see if she was all right. Just about that time the commotion was all over so Cindy told her father what had happened.

About a year ago I knew a boy who would *whistle* every time he saw *lightning*. Because he was frightened he would also shut his *eyelids*. Carrying this fear with him for many years, he finally told me his secret. Doing him a favor, I tried to tell him to be brave. 'Every time a lightning bolt strikes, look right at it,' I said. Fire had killed his brother so this was not an easy thing to do.

'Go on. It won't hurt you,' I persisted. Having a friend seemed to help. It took a little more convincing and finally he agreed to look *straight* up at the next flash.

Just as he looked up, I realised that I now would always *exhibit* a fear of lightning, for he was struck dead at my feet.

With such experiences children became absorbed in the

problem at hand. They realised that they could write uniquely, different from any other student who was working under the same conditions. This recognition and satisfaction in their own personal achievements was apparent as students shared their stories with the class. I felt that this self-awareness was another step toward a healthy creative climate.

The ability to toy with structural elements of language, to be able to juggle words into an orderly fashion, made explorations of the mind arrive at a hunch — the creative seeing — which was a significant way of solving the problem.

Minds would scan the many possibilities of description and then come forth with a solution to the problem of using over ten adjectives to describe a single object.

Pause for our Sponsor

The two-minute comic slap-stick television commercial which advertised a new crackling, rocket-shaped oatmeal cereal was so silly that my three-year old baby brother said he would rather eat dried old spinach leaves than a box full of cereal energy which would shoot brave astronauts unto universal space without the aid of a normal space ship.

Speeders Beware

The tiny black roadster, which looked like a fleeting jungle panther as it sped down the busy interstate highway, came to a sudden screeching halt and choked its last dying breath as it was mangled by the huge loaded moving van which was headed for some distant unknown city.

And how much more challenging to write a description using no adjectives.

The Fish

With tails flashing to and fro, schools of fish headed for streams where they could spawn, leaving behind ripples showing swiftness of movement.

Summer

Summer is books ignored, teachers away, time galore for play and noises until mother can hardly wait for fall to appear.

Books

Books are means of bringing words and pictures to life so that one can experience moods, thoughts and happenings of past, present and future.

To encourage a conscious sense of variety in the choice of wording, I would ask for as many changes as possible in the expression of certain actions.

When given *the boy ran*, children produced the following variations:

The boy jogged
The boy scampered
The boy sped
The boy whizzed
The boy flew
The boy galloped
The boy progressed
The boy hastened
The boy jetted
The boy rocketed
The boy hurried
The boy raced

Then in continuation of the same assignment, I might suggest an adverb be added to each thought so that the reader would have an idea as to how the action was performed.

The boy jogged noisily
The boy scampered wildly
The boy sped rapidly
The boy whizzed freely
The boy flew swiftly
The boy galloped awkwardly
The boy hastened immediately
The boy jetted speedily

The boy rocketed blindly
The boy hurried cheerfully
The boy raced quickly

Many variations of this type of exercise were used with success. Often students would use this as a game for themselves when they had completed their other assignments.

Along with the manipulation of words, students were seeing their progress in the arts of communication. By using a variety of writing games with new imaginative elements we avoided a possibility of repetitive patterns of style or mood among the writings. Yet there were times when requests encouraged a renewal of a certain exercise so that there could be new attempts at the old games.

Naturally from a group of sixth graders many of the papers took on a humorous or gay air. Other assignments seemed to encourage the mysterious. Then there were those tender times when the hidden potential of certain individuals revealed to us the power and intensity of words when mastered with a high degree of consciousness.

Such was a paper by Ann, who had the handicap of deafness. This was her first year in a normal classroom situation. She had learned to understand others by reading lips but was handicapped in conveying her thoughts orally because of a severe speech impediment. The assignment in which each child was to write a paragraph on his or her most desired gift, incorporating a group of spelling words (in italics below) was handled by her in such a skilful way that it brought tears to many eyes.

My Perfect Gift

What is the perfect gift for me? The *chief* thing that I want is to be able to hear well. I wish God had *arranged* my brain so it would make me hear. My brain was damaged *during* my first few days of life, soon after I *arrived* on *earth*. My *parents had hardly known* me when they thought something was the *matter* with me. They began to *search* for the *person* who could help me. The doctors said that they could not make me hear so I am deaf.

How I would love to hear what people say when I *listen!* Oh, God, please repair my brain.

When an assignment was especially enjoyable to an individual, I often found extra stories on my desk. It was satisfying to see that girls and boys were willing to express themselves freely, and most of all that they were acquiring a love for language.

And then there was Music

There once was a hive of musical bees who loved to play poker. These bees were all named after great composers such as Mendelssohn, Bach, Chopin, Beethoven, etc. Well, one day Chopin and the gang were playing a game of cards. (The cards were made by bees because regular cards are too large and the material used in making these cards was pollen.) While they were playing Chopin got a high card and won the game. The card, of course, was called Chopin's Pollen Ace.

And what a store of words are gathered by young people from familiar songs they hear and sing. To make use of this vocabulary I asked for stories which were made from the combinations of song titles.

Once in a While Margie would *Dream* of her *Troubles. Sixteen Going on Seventeen* is quite a problem to *Girls Sweet and Lovely* who are said to be *Born Free* but still have to take orders from *Daddy.*

'*I'm a Believer*', she said to her boy friend, 'in being able to stay up *After the Midnight Hour* on *Monday, Tuesday, Sweet Thursday*, and any other night of the week. But *Never on Sunday* would I expect to be walking *On the Street Where You Live* because I know that you, *Danny Boy*, won't be *Standing on the Corner* on *Sunday.* For after a *Hard Day's Night* you are usually adding to the other *Dreaming* sounds in the *Still of the Night*, and as the *Blue Moon* quietly creeps over the *Beautiful Missouri* in *Gary, Indiana*, I'll too be a *Sleepy Time Gal.*'

. . . and also stories made from book titles.

Three *Little Men* and four *Little Women* with their *Eight Cousins* decided that *They Were Strong and Good* and should go out and seek their fortunes.

'Since *Now We are Six*', said *Pinocchio*, 'we have a quality, some *Call it Courage*, that is more powerful than *The Flying Locomotive*. Let us all bring one important item to help us travel *East of the Sun and West of the Moon*, and to keep us from freezing during *The Long Winter* when *The Wind in the Willows* gets so fierce.

Pandora decided to take *The Magic Fishbone*, which she carefully wrapped in *The Tinder Box*, and *Uncle Remus* thought he would need *The Matchlock Gun* in case he should meet up with *The Biggest Bear*.

The 500 Hats of Bartholomew Cubbins took up too much room so Bartholomew decided to take *The Twenty-One Balloons* instead.

When *The White Cat*, *The Nightingale*, *The Ugly Duckling*, *The Bold Dragon* and all the other friends and supplies were packed for the journey to *Treasure Island*, they all set sail up *The Erie Canal*. After *A Night Ride in A Prairie Schooner* proved to be frightening, *Heidi* said, '*It's Gold* and fortunes that we hoped to find and all we have is *Mosquitoes in the Big Ditch*. Let's go back to *The Little House* on *The Little Island* where we live.'

So they did and were content from that day on reading *The Voyages of Doctor Dolittle* rather than experiencing their own.

*

There were some exercises which were designed in the hope of increasing the powers of vocabulary. In a search for words, students listed in five columns all the words they could think of that started with the letters *t*, *h*, *i*, *n* and *k*. Some would probe their minds, while others expanded their lists by using the dictionary. When the lists were handed in some had as many as five hundred words.

t	*h*	*i*	*n*	*k*
thunder	hymn	ice	north	kilt
tub	husband	instructor	nephew	kite
telephone	habit	inquire	nerve	key
title	home	insult	near	kerosene
take	head	instrument	neat	kept
time	hypochondriac	inch	native	kangaroo
tantrum	hurt	irrigate	neighbor	kiss
tooth	hamburger	ivy	neutral	kitchen
. . . . .	. . . . .	. . . . .	. . . . .	. . . . .
. . . . .	. . . . .	. . . . .	. . . . .	. . . . .
. . . . .	. . . . .	. . . . .	. . . . .	. . . . .

After checking the words for spelling, I underlined one word in each column and told the boys and girls to write a story about any one of the five words underlined. When they had decided on the column from which they would work, they were told to include the other words from the same column which they felt would add interest to their plot.

The key word from the *h* column was *hypochondriac*.

The Wonderful Painkiller

'Oh, my poor aching back,' complained Mrs Hendrix. It hurts almost as much as my left hip. Not to mention my splitting headache. And my stomach! Why it's so nauseated that I feel like I'm going to heave any minute. I think it is just terrible what these hostile people are doing to me.'

'Oh, really, Mrs Hendrix,' her psychiatrist replied calmly, 'and what might that be?'

'Well,' Mrs Hendrix blurted out disgustedly, 'people are always saying I'm a hypochondriac. Little do they know of my hardships and how I hurt all over. I don't know why they would have such ideas. Do you?'

'Oh, no,' replied the doctor quickly, trying to conceal the grin that stole across his face.

'I don't either,' exclaimed the hysterical woman. 'And sometimes they even call me Mrs Hypo! Really,

I get hives all over every time I think of how horrible some humans can be.'

'Calm down, Mrs Hypo . . . Oh, I'm terribly sorry, Mrs Hendrix, but you seem to have quite a case here.'

Dr Higgens leaned back in his chair and started to think. He could see that Mrs Hendrix was a very nice person and could be quite pleasing if she would stop worrying about all her hurts. An ingenious idea suddenly struck him. Mrs Hendrix wasn't really sick. She just imagined she was, so it was her imagination he needed to work on. 'Yes,' he said, 'I think I can help you, Mrs Hendrix. Come back tomorrow and I will have your prescription ready.'

The next day when his patient returned the psychiatrist gave her a bottle of red medicine (which was really just colored water flavored with cherry spices). 'Take a teaspoon of this every day, Mrs Hendrix,' he told her, 'and you'll feel like a new woman.'

So she faithfully followed the doctor's orders and took the medicine every day. When she ran out she happily got some more. Mrs Hendrix never knew she was only taking water and she got so that if she didn't have her medicine she became very ill. But as long as she had her prescription, she no longer had any ailments.

Who would have guessed that water could be habit-forming?

In another story from the same column, *h*, the key word from the student's list was *Hawaiian*. From sixth graders there are bound to be times when the writing products are not the best for class consumption.

Hawaiian Hula

The swinging hip-hugger was on the hefty hips of the slightly heavy Hawaiian girl. She had gone out on the beach, turned on the radio and lain down with her hands and head facing the sand.

Cars streaked along the highway so rapidly that it seemed as though they were hardly there a second.

Then all of a sudden a man with grey hair sneaked up to one of the nearby palm trees. He had his necktie off, but after all it was a hot day, one of the hottest in the history of Hawaii. But was this really the reason? He inched up to the Hawaiian girl with necktie in hand. He lifted it up to his head, slowly, very slowly wrapping it around the neck of the girl, and tightened it . . .

It was stories like this that I would have read to me personally without criticism. Being exposed to television, comics and movies, students are likely to try their hand at the weird and gruesome, but with a continual exposure to the great classics in literature they themselves soon are able to judge the worthwhile from the mediocre.

Besides its use in stories, the vocabulary list served us in another shorter writing game. Since there was no special pattern in making out the list of words other than that they be in five columns and start with the letters *t, h, i, n* and *k,* the children were not concerned about the words as they read across. I now told them to look at the five words that had been written horizontally across the page and use them in a sentence.

The words *thunder, hymn, ice, north* and *kilt* were arranged into this sentence:

> The Scotsman played a *hymn* on his bagpipes as the *north* wind, sounding like *thunder,* blew his *kilt* across the *ice.*

Others were:

> Mrs Brown's *husband* said he would be an *instructor* and show his *nephew* how to fly a *kite* while floating down the river in a *tub.*

> The *night* of the concert he played his *instrument* in such a *horrible* fashion that the *kind* conductor *told* him to take up dancing.

*

Autobiographies can be both fun and revealing. Children were asked to write a story about themselves with no mention of names so that when I read the stories to the class (with their permission) friends could see if they might identify the author. Even with a bit of exaggeration, interests and personalities revealed themselves. For instance in the two autobiographies that follow it would not take a psychologist to work out which child has grown up without a memory of a father, and cherishes the thought of having a dad.

Who, Me?

I was quite shy when I entered this sixth grade class because I came from another school and had not made many new friends. Then came the day when we chose up sides for a baseball game. I am sometimes lost for words, but I am never lost on a baseball diamond and I proved it that day by hitting two home runs. The other boys seemed to be friendlier after that game and I guess I also became a little more relaxed and made some new steps in meeting people.

Besides baseball I find enjoyment in reading. Especially sports stories. When I grow up I would like to be a baseball star, but since this is quite a task, my father has suggested that I go to college just for insurance. (In case I break a leg during a game and am out for a few seasons.)

If you haven't guessed who I am by now I will give you further clues by telling you that I wear size eight shoes, and my mother usually buys me the strangest colors in striped socks. I never carry a lunch box or an umbrella. I don't wear glasses and I eat everything on my tray in the cafeteria, and if you'll share your dessert with me today I'll tell you who I am.

Your Hero

I am a boy with quite a lot of muscles. I have blue eyes and wear fourteen in shirts. I have many girl friends in this room and most of them are crazy about me. (I hope.)

When I grow up I want to go to Harvard and become an anthropologist because I want to know where or what I came from. (Who knows, it could be a rattle-snake.)

Now I want to tell you something of my hobbies. I like girls, football, basketball, and swimming (in the water as well as on the dance floor). I am always a real swinger, and I always find it easy to get into fights with my mother. Probably because she is the opposite sex. She sometimes thinks I am going to be President of the United States. Boy, is she in for some surprises.

I have an older brother. He can beat me at most anything except getting in fights with Mom.

My dad is the neatest thing around. He can take a joke and all that. He never treats me like a baby either.

Now to get to my personality. I have a bad temper and usually get mad at teachers, mothers, and brothers. I can be pretty nice at times and people seem to like me, but wow, can I irritate them when I am so forgetful.

I have a very exciting life, like when I went deer hunting with my father. He saw a deer and went after it. I lost him in the woods and looked for him. I accidentally ran into some wild baby boars but left them alone since I knew the mother must be nearby. And sure enough, I heard a noise and turned around. The mother boar was heading right for me! I looked for a tree but there wasn't one nearby. It was too late anyway because the boar leaped for me and tore at my knee. My father heard my screams and came running to the rescue. He shot the wild boar and the only trophy we have is the scar on my knee.

Before you guess who I am you might like to know that I love to tell stories and they are not always true.

From experience I had seen children limit their written vocabulary for fear of mis-spelling a word. In our exercises spelling was not considered a handicap. Since our goal was to capture the inner thought of each child, we established a system of conveying our message in the best words possible. Then if grammar or spelling skills needed to be emphasised, common mistakes were noted and were covered during a language or spelling period. Skill training during a separate language or spelling period left our creative writing classes free for creativity.

With time permitting, I found it valuable to go over each paper with each child individually. Never would I red pencil an error since I believed that corrections were only meaningful when the student was actively aware of his mistakes. By my encouraging proof-reading of each paper, students found many of their own errors. Because they were told to self-edit in order to find out if they said what they really wanted to say, a great many improvements were made before the paper was ready to be presented to the class.

Chapter Three

GAMES AND ACTIVITIES FOR
CREATIVE THINKING

A WELCOMED CHANGE OF PACE from our regular studies was a number of games and activities which not only offered enjoyment to the class but encouraged creation of spontaneous expression. Once students became confident in taking part in such experiences they released many of their hidden talents. Students who might have a difficult time with arithmetic, science or spelling found security and satisfaction when they were successfully able to match wits with their classmates.

These games also proved helpful as a motivating factor. How effectively time would be spent if there was a possibility of having a puppet show before lunch, or a game of vocabulary baseball before recess.

The greatest asset, however, was the growth in creative expression which evolved from these activities. Children themselves were good listeners as well as eager participants for they realised these games offered them an enjoyable entertainment.

BASKETBALL WITH WORDS

Equipment: Two tag board baskets with slots

Many tag board disks containing words which have come from different areas of the curriculum
Two active teams
Pencils and paper

A team member comes to the front of the room and draws as many disks (representing basketballs) as he wishes from the pile; these are placed face down. If he should draw two balls, he has a chance for two points; three balls could mean three points, etc. Both teams are shown the words on the disks which have been drawn. The students at their seats begin writing a sentence using these words while the drawing member of the first team thinks of his own sentence employing the same words. After a pause so that the writing members have a chance to write their sentences, the team member gives from memory his solution using the words. If he makes a complete sentence using all the words drawn, he puts the disks into the slot of his team's basket. If he is unsuccessful, the disks picked are placed back among the unturned disks and shuffled for the next drawing.

Time out is taken at this point to hear some of the written results even though they have no bearing on the scoring of points.

The game then continues with a shooter from the second team who makes his drawing of words and creates a new sentence.

At the end of the game, the tag board balls are counted in each basket to determine which team has scored the more points.

ADD A WORD OR TWO[1]

This game not only encouraged thought and word powers but seemed to increase the structural fibers of language. Children soon learned how and where to slip in an extra adjective or adverb, and how a conjunction or new verb could give their sentence new meaning.

Each student wrote a simple sentence of no more than three words. This sentence was passed on to a neighbor who would add one or two words to the sentence he received providing it left a complete thought. The work was then passed to another classmate. Students continued exchanging sentences until they felt that they had exhausted the possibilities.

How the class loved hearing the results and picking out their addition from the final accomplishment!

Example:

Tim's first sentence: *The limb broke.*

[1] Two variations of this game, including one for the study of grammar, are described in the Words in Color *Teacher's Guide*; C. Gattegno (Educational Explorers, Reading, 1963).

Alan adds: The *tree* limb broke *yesterday*.

Steven: The *maple* tree limb broke yesterday.

Larry: The maple tree limb broke yesterday *at noon*.

Valerie: *Mother said*, 'The maple tree limb broke yesterday at noon.'

Ann: *Our frightened* Mother said, 'The maple tree limb broke yesterday at noon.'

Linda: Our frightened Mother said *excitedly*, 'The maple tree limb broke yesterday at noon.'

Lisa: Our frightened Mother said excitedly *to Dad*, 'The maple tree limb broke yesterday at noon.'

Brenda: Our frightened Mother said excitedly to Dad, 'The maple tree limb broke yesterday at *high* noon.'

Pam: Our frightened Mother said excitedly to Dad, 'The maple tree limb broke *in half* yesterday at high noon.'

Janny: Our frightened Mother said excitedly to Dad, 'The maple tree limb broke in half *and fell* yesterday at high noon.'

Greg: Our frightened Mother said excitedly to Dad, 'The maple tree limb broke in half and fell *on Patrick* yesterday at high noon.'

Danny: Our frightened Mother said excitedly to Dad, 'The maple tree limb broke in half and fell on Patrick, *our dog*, yesterday at high noon.'

Jeff: Our frightened Mother said excitedly to Dad, 'The maple tree limb broke in half and fell on Patrick, our *brown collie* dog, yesterday at high noon.'

Examples of other attempts:

First sentence: Birds sing.

Final result: Each Spring blue birds sing merrily in the mulberry trees and fly gaily around our house begging food from anyone passing by.

First sentence: He screamed.

Final result: At midnight on Hallowe'en, he screamed and shuddered frantically at the horrible weird figures surrounding him with their long hairy arms and ugly rubber faces.

THE MAGIC BALL OF STRING

Equipment for this game is a magic ball of string which contains a hidden story.

This ball of string has knots tied at various intervals. Some may be two feet apart whereas others may be tied at intervals of as much as five feet. If all boys and girls wish to take part in this game there should be as many knots as there are children.

Normal sitting arrangements may be used or students may sit in a big circle so that the ball can be easily passed.

Start the game off by placing the ball on the floor; then on taking the loose end you begin a story. As you rewind the string and come to a knot, you must stop the dialogue even if in the middle of a sentence, and pass the string on to a neighbor who continues to wind the ball and gather new adventures for the tale until he also comes to a knot. When a new knot appears, a new narrator takes over. The end of the story is revealed as the last of the string is unwound.

For variations of the magic string game you may have a ball of different colors of yarn. Certain colors would signify different moods in the plot of the story. For instance, when green yarn appears, the story must be adventurous; when blue is unwound, the story becomes sad; yellow brings gaity; red tells of excitement; black could reveal the mysterious, etc . . .

PANTOMIME

Besides creating verbal stories, we found that pantomime led to freedom of expression.

A setting would be decided upon, such as a bus station. Then perhaps five students would be chosen to leave the room for one minute and among themselves agree which characters they would portray. As they entered the room they would try to reveal by their walk, motions or behavior who they were. One might be a lost child, another a man late for work, a third an old man with time to waste.

After the short scene the class would describe their interpretations of the roles. The actors and actresses, in turn, would tell them if they were correct in their observations or explain the character they had hoped to portray.

A restaurant scene could develop characters such as a forgetful waitress, a henpecked husband, a poorly mannered boy or perhaps a sophisticated lady.

Other settings which proved interesting were a classroom on the first day of school, a circus, a cinema, the shower room after a losing ball game, a Parent Teacher Association meeting.

PARTY TIME

Balloons mean a party so you can imagine the excitement when children arrive for a day of school and see balloons hanging from the chandeliers. And a party we did have . . . a writing party. For in each balloon was a slip of paper with a character, scene and plot suggestion. As children popped their balloons they found such ingredients as:

Who: Harold
What: Chased by a tiger
Where: Down the main street of town

Who: Captain Strong
What: Without a parachute flying in a plane; motor trouble
Where: Over a barren desert

Who: Princess Pauline
What: Tired of always being prim and proper
Where: On tour with the king and queen

The real fun came when the boys and girls had the opportunity to share their stories with the class.

Princess Pauline

How boring court life had been in the twelve years that Princess Pauline lived at Huntingdon Castle. The same old servants waiting on her hand and foot, a kind but stern governess instructing her on the etiquette of court life, and always the extremes of luxuries everywhere. How she hated her china doll with eyes of real sapphires and lips of red rubies. Her diamond necklace was thrown in the bottom of her drawer. She would have loved to own a necklace of plastic beads like the ones she saw in a fashion magazine.

But alas, 'A Princess must be a Princess'. That is why she wasn't at all excited when the king and queen informed her that they felt she was old enough to accompany them on the year's tour throughout the country.

All the formal dinners and meetings of public leaders were of no interest to this energetic little girl, but she couldn't argue with the king and queen, so she had her servants prepare her for the journey.

The first town was more boring than she had imagined. The royal party stood for hours in a line greeting people. Ugly old men and overly-affected ladies kissed her cheek or patted her on the head. How awful!

The princess knew she couldn't stand many more days like that so she thought of a plan. Everyone wanted to see the royal family, so if she could get Louise, the governess's daughter, to stand in line for her she could take part in more important matters.

Of course, the king and queen were quite shocked when they saw Louise standing in line all dressed up in their daughter's clothes, but they would have been the last to reveal the impostor. How could they explain it to the people?

Meanwhile, the real princess was having a grand time mingling in the crowd and talking to other children. What fun it was hearing of the games they played and the schools they attended. This was the best day of her life.

That evening she thanked Louise for stepping in for her and told her of the great adventures she experienced.

The girls became close friends and whenever Princess Pauline needed a break from the court life, Louise doubled for her.

Life from then on was never boring. Princess Pauline had found a way to escape her patterned life and most of all she had a true friend.

Every classroom has its chief talkers and our boy, Steven, was responsible for introducing a new game which proved to be a good fill-in whenever we had a few minutes before a bell.

One day, as Steven was doing his regular conversing, I suggested that he come to the front of the room and keep talking until he had nothing more to say. Being such an extrovert, Steven loved this opportunity to perform and made the most of it by talking for almost fifteen minutes. He talked of his family, his likes, his pets, his vacation and anything else that came to mind. The children love this spontaneous response and wanted their turn at our new game, *Keep Talking*.

In order to guard against repetition and lack of interest, we developed some rules for our game. To make it more of a challenge we gave the speaker his subject after he came to the front of the room. This was determined by two words, written by any two students on a small slip of paper. For instance, if one child wrote *pumpkin* and another wrote *baseball*, the talker had to develop a story, as his minutes were ticking away, about a pumpkin and baseball.

We gave each story a limit of two minutes, so a timer was selected to let the speaker know when to begin and when to stop talking. The timer also signaled the speaker with his hands when he had but ten seconds left so that he might complete his story. Since some story-tellers would use much of their time in long hesitations, it was decided that a five-second pause, or more than five repetitions of 'an-ah', would disqualify the speaker.

What a stimulus to quick thinking! Students who found it a struggle in their first attempts were anxious for another turn to improve their abilities and soon we had most of the class able to create a story of interest and amusement at random.

How do you do?

A student is introduced with an adjective which blends with his name. He then must repeat his name in a sentence that shows his name fits him and which mentions performing some type of action with another classmate who also is given a descriptive name, who then continues the game.

Steven: I am Sly Steven and I enjoy tricking Aggressive Alan.

Alan: I am Aggressive Alan and would like to beat up Leaping Linda.

Linda: I am Leaping Linda and can jump higher than Bashful Brenda.

Brenda: I am Bashful Brenda and turn pink when I see Sure-footed Sandy.

Sandy: I am Sure-footed Sandy who just tripped over Terrific Tim...

... and on ... and on ... and on.

For variation, make-believe names can be created and anyone who has a good response can raise his hand for a turn at the next introduction.

PUPPETS

With all our acting, there was nothing like our puppet plays to let the children really free themselves from their inhibitions. Since the puppet took on all the characterisation, and the student who was doing the talking and maneuvering was hidden behind a screen, individual fears were usually discarded.

The puppets had been made by each girl and boy during an art period, using a man's sock filled with cotton stuffing. The facial features were formed with buttons, yarn and felt. In the cut-away heel was sewn a mouth of red felt which was manipulated by the fingers and thumb from the inside of the sock.

Students seemed to forget themselves completely as they directed their attentions to making their puppet portray his role effectively, even if the puppet's behavior was in conflict with their own personalities.

Since all of our plays were *ad lib*, no-one had any memorised lines. An allowance of one minute was given to the cast so that they might decide on a plot and who their characters would be.

Tim, our star ball player, who had no time for girls, was as eager as everyone else to have his puppet star in a performance. I remember Tim's first reaction to a romantic scene. When one of the female puppets began to make passes at his puppet, the puppet responded very politely to the advances, but the class was in an uproar for every once in a while we would hear a quiet 'Oh, no' from behind the screen. It was almost as if Tim were ashamed of his puppet's behavior. It so turned out that Tim's puppet was often in demand whenever a plot needed a gallant, suave lover. And this is the way other puppets gained particular personalities. As soon as certain characterisations proved successful, we would see repeats of the same puppet being silly, or vicious, or cowardly. Because students couldn't see their silly Sam acting sensible, Mr Moody, the villain, acting kind, or brilliant Beatrice acting dumb, they needed more characters and began making more puppets at home.

My drawer of extra puppets took on many secondary roles but the children's individual characters which they had created with their sewing and imaginations became so realistic that mothers often had to ask if Clara, Wendell or Agnes were classmates or puppets.

These plays created the same problem as some of our other games. The children enjoyed them so much that we had to put a time limit on each performance. This limit was usually five minutes.

Our screen was always accessible in the room so in a matter of seconds we could be ready for a play. It is indeed surprising how much action and adventure can be covered when children feel free to act and want to make every second count.

Chapter Four

READING FOR BETTER WRITING

IF I WERE TO CHOOSE but one form of stimulus for creative writing it would be exposure to good literature. Here one can find all types of motivations which could act as a bridge between the listening ear and the creative mind. Through books a child discovers new ideas to put into writing in his own creative way. Books are incentives which suggest many styles of writing.

Reading and writing have always been bridged together, but often one forgets to use the connection that is available and can be so profitable in releasing potential output in youngsters. Good books should be accessible to children and time should be allowed for them to read and share their new discoveries. Also it is important to provide a rich listening period where the teacher can present good literature that children would not read for themselves.

When I found our school library without one of my favorite books, *The Little Prince* by Antoine de Saint-Exupéry, I brought my personal copy to school and read it to the class. In the discussion that followed it was evident that the students' sense of values deepened with this reading. So many wished to re-read the book for themselves that our school librarian soon obtained two copies.

The children might never have discovered this book for themselves because they confessed to me that it was one they would not have selected from the shelves on their own. Yet many found it a treasure. One girl, for example, suggested to her parents that they buy her a copy for her birthday.

In order to call attention to other good books, I sometimes set up a display which would stimulate curiosity about certain books or characters. Another technique I used was to have some type of chart which encouraged various types of reading. I displayed a tree with many branches, each of which was labeled. When a book was completed the child made a leaf for the appropriate branch, which might be mystery, historical, science-fiction, adventure, animal or sports.

A book worm, which gained a segment each time a book was read, was another favorite with the class.

Since all children do not read at the same level I tried to set up a plan for each child which would act as a reading ladder. When a child enjoyed a certain book I often had a suggestion for another book which comprised a similar interest but of a better quality. Children needed the experience of moving gradually up the scale. Before the year was ended more than half the class had passed beyond the Nancy Drew and Hardy Boys mysteries and were reading such classics as *Call it Courage*, *Moby Dick*, and *20,000 Leagues under the Sea*.

Besides the school library, there were carefully chosen pocket books from my own personal library which I lent to the students. When a child showed a special interest in a character we had studied in social studies or science, I (being a great lover of biographies) tried to have a point of interest ready which would open the door to some new investigations in the biographical field.

With a wide reading span there was a richer background for writing. Whenever a spark for our creative writing classes was needed, the library shelves seemed to have the answer.

Aesop's Fables ignited the children's imaginations and led them to create their own stories with a moral.

> Betty was continually bragging of how well she could do most anything. Whenever the other girls would try to hit a ball, Betty would show them the proper way to hold the bat. When anyone wanted to play a new game Betty was always there to tell them the rules. One day a neighbor boy got a new horse and asked the girls if they wanted to take a ride. Betty who had never been on a horse before decided that she should be first to show them how to ride. She got on the wrong side of the horse. He threw her and she ended up in the hospital.
>
> Moral: Don't bite off more than you can chew.

One day Henry the Hobo was walking along and met Sam, another hobo from Mexico. 'What are you doing in Texas?' he asked Sam.

'I'm trying to get a job,' answered Sam.

'Who would hire a bum like you?'

'Oh, most any store,' answered the energetic hobo.

The Texan began to laugh and said, 'If you really think you can get a job why don't you go ask in that restaurant right now?'

Sam did and was surprised when the manager answered, 'But of course, I've been looking for a fellow like you to advertise our new Hobo Jelly.'

Moral: Nothing ventured, nothing gained.

It was a cold frosty morning and the lake outside the Cottage Inn was frozen stiff. Mr Bugbee, the inn-keeper, was outside with his son.

'Arnold,' cried Mr Bugbee, 'I want you to put a sign by that spot on the lake that isn't frozen.'

An hour later there was a lovely sign that read *Thin Ice*. The sign was neatly done but Mr Bugbee, who could never give a compliment said, 'Arnold, that sign should be over a little more to the right. I guess I'll have to do it myself.'

As Mr Bugbee stepped out on the ice to get the sign the ice cracked and he fell in the lake.

Moral: Let well enough alone.

An exposure to Paul Bunyan and Pecos Bill[1] made the children eager to create their own forms of exaggerations.

The hurricane was like a newly wound clock ticking its life away.

The hurricane was as wild as a bull being teased.

The hurricane was as timely as Easter eggs in December.

[1] Giant folk heroes of the North American continent.

The dancer was as graceful as a newly born fawn trying to walk.

The dancer was as steady as a two year old on skis.

The dancer moved across the stage like a frog with the hiccups.

The hot rod was as smooth as Apollo on his golden chariot.

The hot rod was as noisy as a flock of geese honking their way South.

The hot rod was as speedy as a boy getting ready for his first little league game.

Similes were a never-ending source of fun.

The day passed so rapidly that it was nearly bedtime before lunch.

The room was so dark that a cat with a flashlight couldn't see.

The book was so dry that a bookworm had to carry a canteen to get through it.

The miniskirt was so short that the scarf around the girl's neck covered it.

His breath was so bad that it evaporated the gargle.

The rocket hit the moon with such force that it knocked it out of orbit.

*

From the joke section of our weekly news magazine we found inspiration from the crazy *Daffynitions*, which were fun to create in spare moments.

A pink carnation — a nation of pink cars

Tooth — something that hurts when it comes in, hurts when it comes out and aches in between

Dog — a flea's best home

Today — yesterday's tomorrow

Bee — a hum bug

Antelope — when two ants run off and get married

Whale — a mammal with a built-in shower

Cat — a walking mousetrap

Light — Edison's brightest idea

Earthquake — a house slipper

*

Even the math book provided a stimulus. After reading numerical equations every day, an eager group of writers decided that verbal examples of mathematical problems might prove interesting.

Apple = red
Banana = yellow
When you eat the two together you have an orange.

An eagle had 197 feathers
A worry causes the loss of 196 feathers
We have a bald eagle.

One quilly porcupine − his quills = a bare skin.

A fisherman fishes
He catches an electric eel
He has a hot rod.

A steak + a pickle + a banana sundae + a shrimp salad + a root beer float + a chocolate cake + a hot dog = indigestion.

A goose with offspring who have offspring = a Granny Goose.

*

Greek myths also were a fertile ground for writing ideas.

The Challenge

Nanerculus was the mightiest hero in the whole world. His protector was the god Dublet. He gave Nanerculus strange powers for smartness and strength.

Nan (short for Nanerculus) went to the friendly oracle in the town, which served free drinks to all, to ask the oracle what he could do. (He was getting very bored with life.)

The oracle suggested he kill Quenlitopod. Quenlitopod was a very dreaded monster. He had hypnotising eyes and could swim like a fish, fly like a bird, and could escape his enemies quickly because of his feet shaped like skis. He even had tentacles that could sting a victim to death and suction cups that would draw out a person's blood.

Boy, this was just the challenge Nan needed. He then asked the oracle where he might find this monster.

The oracle replied, 'Go down Main Street and turn left. Go straight till you're out of town. Follow the river to a cave which is situated on the side of Mt Tasufa. In this cave you will find the monster who waits for anyone who is brave enough to come near.'

Nanerculus followed the directions to the cave. When he got there he tip-toed in to the entrance. As he entered he could see that Quenlitopod was having his breakfast, two ladies sunny side up, three slabs of a cow's side and a barrel of berry juice to drink.

Nanerculus began thinking of a plan. He remembered the bat-belt his Mommy had given him for his birthday. He took out his bat-dynamite and planted it around the cave. He then stepped back behind a rock and watched the fireworks.

This was the end of Quenlitopod, but it just so happens that Quenlitopod was a father, so if Nanerculus ever gets bored again, Tedemont, son of Quenlitopod, will be waiting for him.

*

Because the class had loved the book *Ben and Me*, they enjoyed writing original stories of their imaginative adventures with famous personages.

Leonardo and Me

Mr da Vinci was having all kinds of troubles finding a decent model for his portrait paintings. Every girl he hired would start squirming in her seat and moving around just as he was painting important details. Oh, would he lose his temper. And of course the girls would be fired.

Always being of service, I told him that I could help.

'How can a little ant like you help me?' he asked.

'When you interview the next applicant, I will crawl up her arm and tickle her. If she doesn't move she will make a good model.'

Mr da Vinci, who was getting quite desperate, thought the idea was worth a try.

A well dressed, average looking lady answered our ad. in the *Florence Gazette*. Mr da Vinci told the young lady to have a seat and not to move. Then I went to work. I crawled up her arm and around her shoulders. She just sat there, not moving a muscle.

Mr da Vinci could see that this gal had will-power and began painting.

I was just about ready to disembark from this fair body when I decided to give her one more test. I slowly crawled across her neck. I guess this was too much for her because she gave a little smile just as Mr da Vinci was painting her mouth . . . and from that day on he (not me) was famous for the Mona Lisa smile.

*

Poetry is an area of creative writing in which most teachers like to have their students experiment, but before I had my class do any such writing I wanted them to become familiar with several types of verse. I read them poems regularly from a book of my old favorites, attempting not only to show a variety of styles but also to reveal that poetry could be fun.

Some of our first writing was stimulated in the same way as our first restrictive stories, by tying in three or four key words. Words such as *march*, *autumn*, *soap* and *short* gave us a start, which was enjoyable even though sometimes nonsensical.

There was a *short* month called *March*
That fell in the season of *Autumn*

It happened to be in that year
Lawrence Welk ran out of *soap* bubbles.

When I was a *short* little kid
I'd play in the leaves of *Autumn*
Then my Mom would make me *march*
And wash all over with *soap*.

One day in *Short Autumn*
I was without hope
In a *march* to the bathroom
I slipped on the *soap*.

Always looking for a new stimulating motivation, I was
struck with an idea one morning while listening to a tune on
my way to school. A popular song telling of coloring a picture
certain colors to correspond to different feelings, moods or
situations seemed to be worthwhile to try with sixth graders.
The class was delighted with the results they achieved in their
first experimentation with the limericks which described
(in verse) why to use a certain color in their imaginative
coloring book.

My name is Mac
I live in a shack
I never wash
So paint me black.

I met a handsome fellow
Who thinks I'm very bright
We're planning to be married
So paint me wedding white.

On a trip to Hawaii
I bought a lei
The colors faded
So paint me grey.

Billie and Margie
Have the flu
I have no playmate
So paint me blue.

I am a Martian
Martians are mean
So if you color me
Color me green.

I'm from China
A simple fellow
Who when colored
Is fleshy yellow.

They call me Brain the Owl
My job it is to think
But times when I am foolish
My color's blushing pink.

Love is very funny
And strange as it may seem
Since my boyfriend married
My color is turquoise green.

Our science and social studies units gave us many topics of interest, and after a rich background of words there seemed to be more ease in expressing thought. A science unit on animals gave a clearer background on facts and from this the following verses were created about the creatures studied:

Mr Crab
With an outer shell not at all limp
But firm like a scorpion, or a shrimp
You crawl around on ocean grass
Eating most everything you pass.

Arthropods
It is an ancient insect code
Known by every arthropod
That to be a creature's mate
You must be invertebrate.

Mr Snail
You may be slow in your pace
And wear a very ugly face
But your strength we do admire
Since your home is your attire.

Fly

You spy
With your eye
So where I swat
You are not.

Parasitic Worms

Whether large or small
I dislike worms the most.
They are actually very rude
To feed upon their host.

. . . and with atoms:

Carbon

I am an atom
My name is Kate,
Six is my number
And twelve is my weight.

I have a symbol
The symbol is C
And even with a microscope
You can't see me.

I have no home
I live all around
I live in the sky
And even in the ground.

I am in tree trunks
I am in air
And I'm no bigger
Than a human hair.

When I split up
They call it fission,
I lose my head
In the big collision.

When there seemed to be a struggle for a writing vocabulary
I suggested that children write all of the words that came to

mind before trying to compile their thoughts. In an assignment where the subject was to be a clock, a list of compiled words (no matter how small it might be) seemed to help trigger the action.

Words collected:
    time   hands   numbers   round   circle

The Clock

The clock tells time.
It moves.
It points to numbers
That go in circles
Big and small.

Words collected:
    a.m.   p.m.   hands   numbers   day   night

The Clock

The clock has hands and numbers,
To tell time you have to know the
   Difference between
   a.m. and p.m.,
   Night and day.
Anyone can do this if they
   Know numbers,
   Know when to go to bed
   And get up.
It is usually taught to children
   When they are young
But some grown-ups get confused.

The Japanese *haiku* prove to be especially suited to sixth graders. These three-line verses, which have five syllables in the first line, seven in the second and five again in the third line, proved to be another interesting challenge after our many attempts at restrictive writings. With a background of the meaning, subjects and history of the haiku and its place in Japanese literature, the children put much careful thought into these writings.

46

Red, orange, golden leaves
Always fall on Autumn days
This is how Fall is.

Spring with little birds
Makes work for mother robin
To make a good nest.

Winter with snowflakes
Each a little different
Gather on the pines.

Robins, sparrows, jays
Going south for the winter
Coming back in spring.

Birds flying through air
Leaves are growing on trees
Summer must be here.

Brown leaves on the ground
The breeze full of wind and dust
Fall is here at last.

Oceans of icebergs
Mountains of beautiful snow
Winter's real white glow.

*

School newspapers with their new articles, personal inter-
views, student opinion column and team sports are wonderful
experiences in the more serious and informative writings.
When the class put out such a paper for the school it was
evident that the more treasured jobs in reporting were those
that allowed for a bit more of the imaginative slant of the news.

Since no paper would be complete without a column of
advice for the troubled, our 'Dear Winnie' answered the
letters that came from the student box. A box was posted in the
cafeteria so that other classes would have the opportunity to
present their questions. Winnie was in reality a group of three
students who put their heads together to come up with a
solution to each problem.

Dear Winnie,

When I am doing my school-work my neighbors seem to just happen to be strolling by so they say they are going to stop in for a minute. The minute usually turns into an hour. I don't want to be rude and tell them to leave but I do want to keep up my grades. What can I do?

Bothered

Dear Bothered,

It wouldn't be rude if you would just tell your friends the situation and kindly invite them over at a time when you are free.

Winnie

Dear Winnie,

When my teacher asks me a question I feel so embarrassed that I give the wrong answer even though I know the right one. I feel this is lowering my grade. What should I do?

Embarrassed

(P.S. I know you won't print this.)

Dear Embarrassed,

Why don't you participate in class discussions more and this may help you overcome this fear of speaking out.

Winnie

Dear Winnie,

I have two friends. I like them both very much but they dislike each other. All three of us can't play together. When I play with one the other friend gets mad. What shall I do?

Peacemaker

Dear Peacemaker,

You might smooth matters by saying nothing but pleasing things about each girl to the other girl and maybe they can come to realise each other's good qualities. The main thing is not to get involved in their disputes.

Winnie

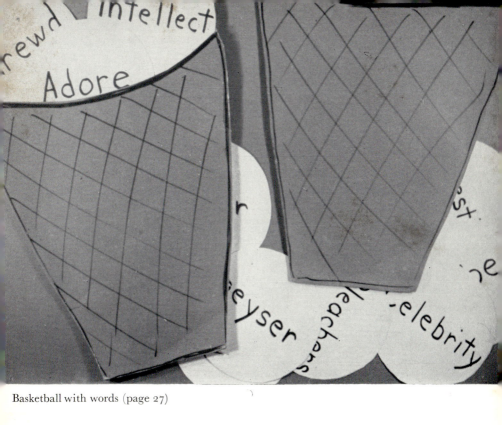

Basketball with words (page 27)

Puppets (page 34)

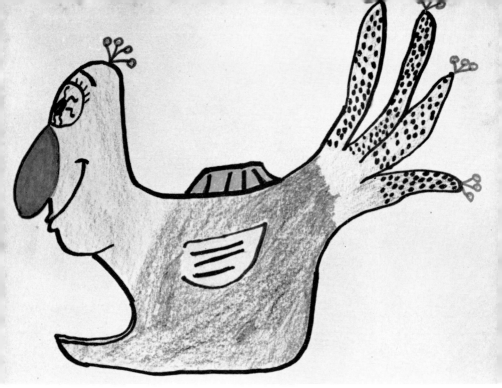

The challenge (page 40)

Newspaper headlines (page 50)

The newspaper seemed to spark many new interests when we studied our local *Arizona Republic*, which we did by having thirty copies delivered to our class every day for two weeks.

One article which naturally caught the eye of the girls, who are at the age of showing interest in new clothing fads, was:

Jersey Isle Declares War on Miniskirts

St Helier, Channel Islands (AP)—Jersey, Britain's honeymoon island in the English Channel, has declared war on miniskirts.

Two girls, one 15 and the other 13, reported they were taken to a police station yesterday and ordered drop their hemlines after a woman officer found the skirts were 8 inches above the knee.

Here, I realised, was the lead for a new form of writing. 'Imagine you are one of the girls or you were there when the girls were taken to the police station. Can you, in story form, rewrite this episode?' . . . and rewrite it they did.

Jane beamed at Judy as they strutted out of the department store in their new mini outfits. But as they rounded the corner of Jersey's busy avenue they lost their elegant strut, for they were approached by a matronly officer of the law who whisked them off to the police station where they were given instructions on the proper apparel for conservative cads.

Other newspaper articles followed in providing a background for our make-believe situations.

*

Advertisements which are overly exaggerated sometimes prove effective. Our young newspaper writers were shown a photograph of an odd looking gadget with all kinds of arms and devices, which was taken from the pages of *Life* magazine. They were told to write the script for an advertisement which would make every reader feel that he must have one of these wonderful 'things'.

Did you lose the rodeo because of a worn out pony? Get a spirited horse reviver which brushes, massages and hammers sense into your animal, all with a flick of the button.

See it at your local stable.

Ask for *Ole Nellie's Automatic Horse Reviver.*

Are you a do-it-yourself man?

No longer do you need to struggle endlessly over a leaky faucet, a broken chair, a worn out television set or the hundreds of other jobs that our *Service Sam* can do for you.

As Service Sam does the work you can relax.

Service Sam Enterprises carries the Goodrepairman's seal of approval.

*

The newspaper headlines served us in another writing project. Words were clipped from headline banners and pasted on a piece of red tag board. By rearranging these words, the children created new headlines:

More Scandal Confusion

Fire Suspends Vacation

Teen-Driving Crack-Down

Noble Grandmother Found

. . . and from these headings came the beginnings of our stories.

Noble Grandmother Found

Baroness Beatrice Von Horne, 88, the sole heir to the Sondinian dynasty, was found yesterday in the little village of Barel on the Southern coast of Nowedian. She was traced to that area through years of research.

All through the continent of Eurena, rare coins from the royal mint of Sondinia were showing up in the various candy shops. Mr Matterburn, a Sondinian official, began the search in 1957. By tracing the path of the royal coins, he was directed to the village of Barel.

No-one in Barel could give him any information on

Baroness Beatrice Von Horne, but he was told of a strange woman in town who waddled through the streets eating chocolates. He knew that his search had ended.

The Baroness was discovered in a peppermint shop, as she was having a little trouble getting through the narrow doors, since she had gained 206 pounds during her twelve years' absence.

Her return to Sondinia was a cause for rejoicing. In her honor the candy merchants erected a six foot chocolate statue of their ruler, which she will be munching on for years to come.

Chapter Five

THE OPPORTUNE MOMENT

BACKGROUND is so valuable in the preliminaries of creative writing and only too often do we let a richly stimulating discussion slip by without taking advantage of its possibilities in the writing program. That is why I felt it so important to be aware of the opportune moments when interests were high. The stimulus that made children write vividly one day might fade if postponed for a future lesson. There were, however, occasions when time would not allow for an immediate writing period, so I might tell them that we should give this topic more thought and possibly consider it for our next writing period, hoping that they would be looking for new ideas and not be forgetting the lesson at hand, or lose interest.

Our letters to Mr Peacock were inspired by a conversation which followed one morning when I told the class that our two pet peacocks were attacked by two dogs. I also told them how funny one cock looked without his beautiful tail and furthermore that he even acted differently.

'Why, I can imagine,' said one girl, 'he has lost his most prized possession.'

'He must be embarrassed,' said another.

'What happened to the dogs?'

'How long will it take to grow new tail feathers?' someone asked.

One question followed another, some of which I couldn't answer. I said, 'Why don't you write a letter with some of these questions, or maybe you could even offer some advice to the poor bird that was mangled?'

Many different approaches were attempted, and all were rather successful since they came from the magic treasure chest of words which were thoughtfully conjured up by each curious mind.

Dear Mr P. Cock,

As a fellow peacock I would like to thank you for starting that neat new fad. Every peacock in town has cut off his tail and I want you to know that we are giving you full credit for the new styles.

Why, I always thought my beauty was only skin deep and I'm excited to find that it goes deeper! My body is much more elegant than I ever imagined.

Thank you again for creating this new sensation. Why, we are even thinking of erecting a statue to you in the barnyard.

Sincerely yours,
A. Bare Peacock

Dear Mr Peacock,

I am sorry to hear of the mishap last Saturday afternoon. I understand that you and two companions were attacked by two dogs. I also am aware of the great loss to your prestige. As my client I feel that I can safely say we shall have a good case in court. In the meantime I advise you to go to the store and buy some artificial feathers so that you are not teased by your neighbors.

Your lawyer,
Mr C. B. Dover

Dear Mr Peacock,

I am very sorry to hear about your accident. I know how embarrassing it must feel being without your tail feathers.

I know of a peacock who had a similar problem and he solved it by trying Flair's Fair Feather Fluid. By applying it to the bare area he had a beautiful new crop of feathers in four days.

I suggest, Mr Peacock, that you buy a bottle. Good luck.

Sincerely,
Mr Alan Roberts
From B. B. B. Co.
(Bird Brain Birds)

Dear Mr Peacock,

I must say your tail feathers looked very tempting to me and my friend Rover last Saturday, but now after a week of spitting out feathers I must say we have learned our lesson: All that's flashy doesn't taste good.

If you are interested in having any of these darn things back, let us know. We have two pillows full of them.

A wiser pair of dogs,
Rover and Spot

BLACKOUT

The New York City blackout caused by electrical failure became a topic of interest with all of the unusual circumstances in which people found themselves. After a discussion of some of these happenings the students were pretty much aware of how dependent our age has become on electrical power. So they were ready to turn on their imaginations and describe the experience they had when the electrical failure hit their town.

There I was, all doped up, ready for my first major surgery. The nurse had wheeled me into the operating room and I could see the blurred image of the surgeon putting on his gloves.

Semi-conscious, I could not hear what was being said, but I knew that it was time for the great surgeon to go to work. It was his job to find my mother's contact lens which had lodged somewhere in my throat when I swallowed it. (Of course, I would have never put it in my mouth if it hadn't fallen into the mashed potatoes.)

I heard a snip, snip, snip. Although I could feel no pain I was aware of the fact that my flesh was being cut. Just then I heard the doctor scream, 'Light! More light!'

There was a scramble of feet around the room as if everyone had a shot of panic. Then I heard another word I care not to repeat, but I could tell from it that the doctor was angry.

Someone finally showed up with a flashlight and a lantern and the surgery continued without a word.

When I woke up the next day, Mother had her contact lens and a'th I th'aid goo monin, I wealithed my boice ad changed.

*

Daylight saving time is a new adjustment to students, especially when they do not fully comprehend the reason and benefits of such a change. So when children came to school on the first morning after the clocks had been turned back there were a number of stories and questions regarding the time change — hence a new opportunity for story writing.

The topic: The effects of daylight saving time on their own special characters.

> Mr Pepper the milkman forgot to set his alarm clock back for daylight saving time.
>
> The milk was delivered late when . . . Mr Pepper the milkman forgot to set his alarm clock back for daylight saving time.
>
> Mrs Brown didn't have milk for breakfast when . . . the milk was delivered late when . . . Mr Pepper the milkman forgot to set his alarm clock back for daylight saving time.
>
> Johnny Brown went to school cranky when . . . Mrs Brown didn't have milk for breakfast when . . . the milk was delivered late when . . . Mr Pepper the milkman forgot to set his alarm clock back for daylight saving time.
>
> Mrs Jones, the teacher, was angry and broke her glasses when . . . Johnny Brown went to school cranky when . . . Mrs Brown didn't have milk for breakfast when . . . the milk was delivered late when . . . Mr Pepper the milkman forgot to set his alarm clock back for daylight saving time.
>
> The arithmetic papers were all corrected wrong when

. . . Mrs Jones the teacher was angry and broke her glasses when . . . Johnny Brown went to school cranky when . . . Mrs Brown didn't have milk for breakfast when . . . the milk was delivered late when . . . Mr Pepper the milkman forgot to set his alarm clock back for daylight saving time.

The class thought that 31 minus 22 was 7 when . . . the arithmetic papers were all corrected wrong when . . . Mrs Jones the teacher was angry and broke her glasses when . . . Johnny Brown went to school cranky when . . . Mrs Brown didn't have milk for breakfast when . . . the milk was delivered late when . . . Mr Pepper the milkman forgot to set his alarm clock back for daylight saving time.

On the 22nd of May the class figured they had 7 more days till the end of school, which was to be the 31st when . . . the class thought that 31 minus 22 was 7 when . . . the arithmetic papers were all corrected wrong when . . . Mrs Jones the teacher was angry and broke her glasses when . . . Johnny Brown went to school cranky when . . . Mrs Brown didn't have milk for breakfast when . . . the milk was delivered late when . . . Mr Pepper the milkman forgot to set his alarm clock back for daylight saving time.

No-one showed up for the last two days of school when . . . on the 22nd of May the class figured they had 7 more days till the end of school, which was to be the 31st when . . . the class thought that 31 minus 22 was 7 when . . . the arithmetic papers were all corrected wrong when . . . Mrs Jones the teacher was angry and broke her glasses when . . . Johnny Brown went to school cranky when . . . Mrs Brown didn't have milk for breakfast when . . . the milk was delivered late when . . . Mr Pepper the milkman forgot to set his alarm clock back for daylight saving time.

The class loved daylight saving time when . . . no-one showed up for the last two days of school when . . . on the 22nd of May the class figured they had 7 more days

till the end of school, which was to be the 31st when
. . . the class thought that 31 minus 22 was 7 when . . .
the arithmetic papers were all corrected wrong when
. . . Mrs Jones the teacher was angry and broke her
glasses when . . . Johnny Brown went to school cranky
when . . . Mrs Brown didn't have milk for breakfast
when . . . the milk was delivered late when . . . Mr Pepper
the milkman forgot to set his alarm clock back for
daylight saving time.

Being creative means being aware. From a science project on
the senses, group work was done in the fields of touch, taste,
hear, smell and see. Each group was secretly to make a box of
objects which would give the rest of the class the opportunity
to test the senses and hence enable them to compile their
findings in a descriptive sentence or two.

The *touch* box, filled with bits of clay, cooked macaroni,
plastic toys, straw and the buds from bolls of cotton gave the
following impressions:

Soft as rubber
Firm as wood
This box is handy
If you should
Need something to carry in your pockets.

I wouldn't want to be hungry if I were presented
with a dish of this chewy stew, but if I need something
to patch the hole in my bicycle tire this box might come
in handy.

The *hear* box contained packages of bubble gum, and as the
box was shaken, thoughts whirled.

I might find this box a necessity if I were stuck on
a desert island. The ingredients could be used to signal
to over-flying planes and keep away the sharks.

Sounds as if a handful of surprises from this package
would make the 4th of July noisier.

The *smell* box was stuffed with a cloth which had been soaked in fingernail polish remover, vaseline, vinegar and lemon oil.

> My mother rubs the very same formula on my chest when I have a cold. That is why I am never sick.

> Our house smells like this when my sister is trying to whip up a new recipe in the kitchen and my older brother is in the bathroom getting ready for a slick date.

For an experiment in *seeing*, strange pictures were flashed rapidly on the overhead projector with the result that the students were not too sure of what was seen.

> Sorry, but I had a bad night and I'm seeing moving spots before my eyes.

> In the picture I saw a flock of geese trying to head south, but they were not making much progress because of the heavy smog.

To *taste*, each student (with eyes closed) was given a cookie which had cracked wheat, hot peppers, garlic salt, Worcestershire sauce, cheese, celery and shredded cabbage added to the dough.

> A meal in itself. Good for someone on a diet. Healthy because of its protein. Appetising because of the tangy flavor . . . but no more, please.

> Every disaster kit should have one. After such a treat, who would mind dying?

From our study on senses also came poetry. Students were asked to examine closely one of the five main senses and to write.

To Feel — Friend or Foe

I like to feel the mud that slides beneath my barefoot toes,
I like to feel the raindrops that spill across my nose.

I love to sit beside the fire and feel its friendly heat,
But screams I shout, when I feel a bee sting at my feet.

I like to feel the collar on my mother's soft fur coat,
I like to feel the coolness, while in the pool I float.

I like to feel the horse's trot as I bounce, high in saddle,
But the feel's not so good, when from my daddy's paddle.

The sense of touch is something I would never be
   without.
But when I know it's going to hurt I'd like to throw it
   out.

To Hear

Without my ears I could not hear
The names that I am called.
But with them I can always say
'Same to you, you all.'

*

The school custodian was nice enough to save thirty card-board boxes for one of our art projects. These boxes were of all sizes and shapes and since they took up so much room they were the topic of interest for the day. 'Now what?' the children asked. When it was time for art, all were curiously awaiting a new adventure. Each child was given a large piece of butcher paper and told to decorate his box as a fancy gift using paints, crêpe paper, paste-ons or any other material which would make for a work of art.

This new experiment was quite successful and with thirty beautiful packages around our room it looked like a party . . . but where was the party? Maybe we could create one. (This is one of the advantages of working with a staff of teachers who are not too shocked by an interruption of the daily schedule. Since spontaneity, to me, is one of the most enjoyable aspects of teaching, we often find ourselves sharing something with our neighbors and they with us.) Each child picked up a box. We walked into a fourth grade room unannounced and sang 'Happy Birthday' to the class, put our packages down and left.

The teacher saw this surprise visit as an 'opportune moment' to do some writing. Since all of the children were anxious to see what was in each package, she decided to put their imaginations to work.

Each child was given a package, which he could tell was empty once he held it. But by using magic they could see all types of new things, and from a world of make-believe came a gamut of wishes which were carefully described on paper.

When this fourth grade class had made use of the boxes they delivered them to another room in the same manner. Then they were taken to another. Teachers soon got wind of the circulating magic boxes and requested their turn in having them delivered.

These boxes, which started out as nothing more than an art project, found their way to more than a dozen classrooms which used them for a writing opportunity. The boxes came to their end as a touring party when a group of first graders could not part with their surprises after having written their stories. My class received the satisfaction of hearing these first graders read their stories as they clutched their precious presents. It was also pleasing to the sixth graders to know how far their boxes had traveled.

COMMUNIST DAY

While studying the Soviet Union in social studies we had access to a film which showed the differences between democratic and communistic ways of life. The students in our Room 26, who had experienced pretty much of an open feeling in the forming of their own opinions, thought it might be fun to have a day of school under rigid communistic techniques.

The next day when the class arrived, they found a Russian flag at the front of the room and on the chalkboard was our slogan:

Speak only when spoken to.

The first announcement over the loud speaker was from the principal, who had been informed of our project. He announced that our class had been selected as the model class for the day and would be last to go into the cafeteria, since the State food supply would be limited on that day. After thanking him for the honor of being selected, I could see by the students' faces that they were already beginning to think the idea might not be so much fun. By the time they had experienced the strict disciplines of our motto, and had been ignored when expressing their own opinions, their appetites were ready for our creative writing. In their assignment they were to write a paper telling why they were happy to be living in a communist country.

Some of the different forms of satire that evolved from this lesson made me wonder if we might have the makings of some new George Orwells in the room.

A True Comrade is a Man's Best Keeper

Why should we not associate with Capitalists? The answer to this question is very obvious and elementary. Our country and government are superior! We do not wish to clutter our minds with the ideas of the Capitalists. They seek to take young minds and destroy them by expecting young people to think for themselves.

Our country has become great because of our unique system of sharing. We are so fortunate to have great leaders who divide the food and money equally. No-one will starve under this superior plan once it gets properly organised. (Maybe next year.) In the United States many people are stricken with poverty and dying of hunger. Then there are those who have strong backs and strong minds and live in mansions and eat caviar, just because they are able to keep what they work for. With our method, everyone is equal. Our superiors, who are always right, tell us that some day everyone in our country will be rich.

We are trying to make the United States turn to our way of life, but they insist on having their precious 'freedom'. What do they know of freedom? And who needs it, anyway?

Do you remember that American hero who once said, 'Give me liberty or give me death!'? This statement only shows the ignorance of the Americans and their beliefs.

In Russia we say, 'Give me Communism or I will die of starvation!' We Russians would rather fight than switch! And we are going to do just that until the whole world sees it our way.

*

With vacation time drawing near, there were dreams of faraway places; and with almost a year's study of the Eastern Hemisphere even those who had no hopes of traveling had a good background in which to create a travel story.

These were written by using the first letter of each sentence to spell out the vacation area of their choice.

Hawaii

*H*ow many years I have dreamed of a trip to the islands! *A*lways wanting to know how to surf, I thrilled at the thought of seeing the ocean waves roll in. *W*here else could I get such a wonderful opportunity?

*A*unt Elsie said she would see to it that I have proper instruction in surfing when I arrive. *I* am pretty good on a skate board, so am hoping this talent will help. *I*n case it doesn't, you may see me returning on a stretcher.

Denmark

*D*ad didn't let us know of our summer plans until last week. *E*ven he didn't realise that we would be able to go until he found out if the boss would give him enough time off from work. *N*ever before had Dad requested a long vacation, so I guess it was only fair that he should have one this year.

*M*y, how much day-dreaming I've done since I heard. *A*ll night I sat up reading tales from Hans Christian Andersen. *R*eading also of different areas in the country, I hope to become more familiar with some of the sights we may see. *K*in folks will be waiting for us in Copenhagen so we will have experienced guides.

Chapter Six

HOLIDAY FUN

HOLIDAYS OFFER new opportunities in writing. With the many traditions come new inspirations. Children come to school with a varied background of holiday activities and past experiences. From these they were able to create new materials in writing and expand their thoughts by sharing with their classmates.

HALLOWE'EN

Hallowe'en was the incentive for many ghost stories told with the magic ball of string (see Games and Activities, page 30) as well as some poetic wizardry. Spooks and goblins seem to be a favorite for children and can be inspired by strange pictures of the weird and fantastic.

Hallowe'en
Witches sailing through the sky,
On their broomsticks, way up high,
Black cats howl as they go by,
For this is Hallowe'en.

Jack-o-lanterns big and round
On each gate post can be found;
Ghosts and goblins all around
For this is Hallowe'en.

Who's Scared?
Witches riding through the night
On their brooms so shiny bright
Owls sitting in a tree,
Who's scared?
Not me!

Goblins prowling,
Wolves are howling
Through the darkness you can't see.
Who's scared?
Not me!

THANKSGIVING

At Thanksgiving time the children had a chance to express gratitude for the good things of life. Some, when asked what they were most thankful for, wrote about our country, their families and homes. Others gave thanks for their good fortune in having certain comforts of life.

Excerpts from these papers give an idea of their thoughts.

> . . . When I drive across the desert, I am so happy that we have an airconditioned car, and give thanks that the pioneers had enough energy to make it across the hot desert to settle in this beautiful oasis.

> . . . I look around and see all of the many different people who are mothers and fathers. Then I am so happy that God put me in the family he did.

> . . . There are some guys who can't enter in our games because of an illness or accident. I feel so sorry for them and I'm thankful that I have a healthy body which can run, jump and play.

CHRISTMAS

At Christmas everyone likes to write a letter to Santa. That is, everyone but sixth graders who would have considered it kid stuff without some type of challenge. The challenge here was to start each sentence of the letter with either the first letter of their first or last name. This was enough to make them intrigued with the make-believe Santa, and they set to work developing their thoughts in a variety of colorful ways.

> Dear Santa,
> Just to inform you what I want for Christmas I have decided to write this letter.

64

opposite Exaggerated advertisements (page 49)

Watch out for Walley (page 77)

Jellybeans are my favorite kind of candy, so would you please fill my stocking with some, Santa? Jump ropes and dolls are things that you bring me every year, but I suppose we'd better keep up the tradition, so please send me a red jump rope this year and a pretty doll.

Jealousy crept all over me last year because you gave Mary a pretty blue coat, so if you wouldn't mind, could I have one this year?

Just one more thing: I would like records of some Christmas carols. *Jingle Bells* is my favorite. Jazz records are okay, too, if you happen to have some neat ones.

Jumping catfish, I didn't know it was getting so late and I have to go to bed so I'll keep up my good record.

Joyfully yours,
Julie

Dear Santa,

Would you please come to my Christmas party? We're going to have a blast and we wanted you to get in on the fun. We've been planning the party for weeks and hoping you would be our special surprise.

We are going to have candy, cake, soft drinks, pizza and all sorts of other goodies. Will you bring a stereo phonograph so we can play records? Why don't you also bring your sleigh? We have a big flat roof on the top of my Dad's studio which would make a good landing dock.

Waiting to hear from you . . .

Willingly yours,
Wayne

Dear Santa,

Before I tell you what I want this year, I want to thank you for the stuffed animal you gave me last year.

Being a lover of horses, I would like a real white horse. But since I can't have one because I have no place to put him, I would like a stereo. Besides, you probably wouldn't have the horse I want. Because you

65

see, I want a white Arabian Albino that comes from a good breed of runners and jumpers.

Believe me, Santa, I've been a pretty girl this year so don't let me down.

Bye bye now,
Barbara Ann

Dear Santa,

Looking back over this past year, I seem to have been an angel. Last year I was pretty good but not as good as I was this year.

Let me tell you some of the things I want. Lions would be nice to keep my brothers away from my room when I have friends spending the night with me. Liking music, I could use a linnet bird to sing me to sleep. Little ones will be okay. Lotion for my hands which are red and rough from doing so many dishes is a necessity.

Los Angeles is where I am going to be spending my Christmas, so be sure you bring the gifts there.

Leaving our house is going to make me very sad because I can spy on you from behind the piano and you don't even know I'm there.

Lots of luck on your long voyage and a Merry Christmas to you and the family.

Leaving love,
Lois

THE NEW YEAR

New Year's resolutions were written by students. I kept these for three months and then returned them to their owners.

This year I am going to try to do my homework without being told. I will set aside a study period and then not get distracted by television during this forbidden time.

I am going to make all my customers on my paper route happy by delivering their papers on time. I am also going to try to get at least ten more subscribers.

My resolution is to earn enough money on my own for a new bicycle. I will do this by helping Dad, mowing lawns and doing odd jobs for neighbors.

When the papers were returned, months later, the boys and girls were both amused and surprised to see how they had managed in keeping their rules for the year.

Another activity for early January was in foreseeing the future. A prediction (of a non-personal nature) in things they wished to see happen during the year was expressed.

The war in Viet Nam will end by the North and South becoming one country and not allowing foreigners to enter.

A pill will be invented which will satisfy the stomach for a whole day, so no-one in the world will die of starvation.

Man will land on the moon and start a settlement.

The Hawthorne Hawks, by winning the city baseball tournament, will get a free trip to Disneyland.

Batman and Robin will catch the Joker for the last time.

Valentine's Day

A Valentine's Day greeting to one's pet seemed to be well directed to a sixth grader's heart.

Dear Pruett,
    When I'm at school you always wait
    Even sometimes, when I'm slow.
    You and I, we communicate,
    More than any friend I know.

Dear Gus, my dog,
    To me you're tops
    To me you're best
    To me you're greater
    Than all the rest.

Using the letters V A L E N T I N E as introductory letters of words to make a complete sentence proved to be quite a challenge.

Vigorous Andy laughingly entertained nine tiny Indians not elephants.

Vultures always leave evidence near the island named Errie.

Valiant armies love enlarging new turmoils into national events.

Virtuous artists let everyone nab their important new engravings.

EASTER

Each student during an art period was given a piece of butcher paper and access to numerous colorful accessories to decorate the Easter bonnet they were about to make. From paint, crêpe paper, yarn, construction paper, buttons, string and other collected items came so many interesting creations that we decided to have an Easter parade. In preparation, everyone was given a few minutes to think of a way to describe their new original for the style show which we presented to one of the neighboring classrooms.

Among the presentations were hats of all sorts:

A hat which is the coming fad in London. Notice the long strands of material which can give you an appearance of a Beatle cut while your hair is growing out.

Here is a hat for the forgetful teacher. Scissors, pencil, eraser, rubber bands, paper-clips, everything the teacher may need right at the fingertips.

Every lady will feel elegant in this Paris original which gives you your own flower garden on top of your head, and these flowers don't need watering.

You've heard of the mini-skirt. Well, now we have the mini-hat. If you can't quite see it, look closely under the front bangs.

MOTHER'S DAY

Mother's Day Game

From our science and social studies units and from current events, names of famous mothers were listed but not shown to the class.

A child was selected and a card with the name of one of the mothers was pinned on his back. The rest of the class were shown the name and told to write three descriptive words that would best describe it. Then the chosen student would start asking questions in turn, which could be answered 'yes' or 'no'. When a 'yes' answer was gained, the questioner received *one* of the descriptive words as a clue.

For instance, Madame Curie could be the name pinned on the back. The class might write clue words such as Pierre, scientist, radium, Poland or Paris.

If the questioner asked, 'Is the person now living?', the answer would be 'No'. He would then have to move on to the next person with his next question.

If, however, the question had been, 'Is the person dead?', the answer would be 'Yes'. The person who was asked the question would then read one of the clue words on his paper, which might say *radium*, before the questioner went on to the next person with his next question. When he felt he knew the name of the mother, he could end the questioning. The winner was the student who could name his mother with the least number of questions.

Some of the other mothers used in this game were Doris Day, Martha Washington, Jackie Kennedy, Cleopatra, Eleanor Roosevelt and Mamie Eisenhower.

This game also proved to be a good review when we broadened the scope to include all famous people. For variety we might include events, book characters or famous places.

It takes all kinds of mothers to make conversational paragraphs tingle with excitement. In a situation of eleven-year-old

Lucille Ball's mother trying to brief her daughter on how to act in a restaurant, we get the following rules of etiquette:

'Now Lucy, we are going to try again to see if you are ready to take out in public. Remember, you don't use your fork to shoot spitwads across the room, and the fingerbowl is to wash you fingers, not your whole face. And please, please, don't ask the waiter to tell you what is in each dish you order. We don't have time for all that.

'I didn't bring your bib, Lucille, so I wish you hadn't ordered that Italian spaghetti.

'I know, I know, you like it because it looks like worms. You don't need to tell me again.

'What? You found a real worm in the sauce? Oh, Lucille, honey, don't eat another bite. I'll call the waitress.

'Waitress! Waitress! What are you trying to do, kill my little girl by feeding her worms?

'What did you say? You were only fooling? Well, I'm not fooling. Come, Lucille, let's have a talk in the ladies' room.'

. . . and then Cassius Clay's mother tries to tell him that he can't have the new bike he was looking forward to owning.

'Sorry, Cassius, but I told you if you got into one more fight this week you were not going to get a thing more from me.

'So you think you can get your own bike. Well, I'm telling you now, you are going about it the wrong way. What can anyone prove with his fists?'

Wham! Slap! Crack! Boom!

'That was for not getting home on time.'

Wham! Bang! Bash!

'And that for letting that Puggy Powers beat you up. When are you going to act like a man and learn to defend yourself? Until you do, no new bicycle!'

*

These were two of the many poems that were unassigned, but were written for the one person who was an inspiration for every child. They were sent home to be included with Mother's Day gifts, and it is probable that these sincere tributes were more appreciated than the gifts themselves.

What Would We Do Without Mother?

Mother, would you make my bed,
And hang up all my clothes?
Oh, and Mom, if you don't mind
Please drive me over to Joe's.

Mother, help me curl my hair,
I can't seem to do it right.
And Mom, please try to finish
My new Easter dress tonight.

Hey Mom! What's for dinner?
Has the turkey yet been carved?
What! You haven't fixed it yet?
Well hurry up, I'm starved.

Mom, it's awfully hot today
Even in the shade
And I'm so very thirsty
Please fix some lemonade.

Mother would you iron this blouse?
I simple have to have it!
And Mom, while I'm away at camp
Please feed my new pet rabbit.

A Mother is a chauffeur,
A Mother is a maid.
A Mother is a royal chef
Who is never justly paid.

To the many laws of science
I would like to add another
'Behind every happy boy and girl
Is an understanding Mother!'

My Mother

M is for *magnificent* which she is in every way
O is for *opportunities* she gives me every day
T is for the *tenderness* she shows when I am sad
H is for the *hug* I get when I make her glad
E is for just *everything* I don't have room to name
R is for the *rarity* of her unknown fame.

*

Mothers cover such a large range of activities and bring such varied responses that the unfinished sentence

Mothers are for . . .

proved to be a successful attempt in our creative writing.

> Mothers are for seeing that you don't wear your plaid shirt with your polka-dotted trousers.

> Mothers are for reminding you of all the things you forgot to do so that when you forget the next time you'll know what you should have remembered.

> Mothers are for easing Dad's temper when you bring home your report card.

As mentioned in the section on the opportune moment, an occasion where interest is high is the right time to step in with creative writing. Holidays automatically offer this opportune moment, and its use in the most beneficial manner can further the literary growth of students.

Chapter Seven

A PICTURE BRINGS A THOUSAND WORDS

A PICTURE CAN TELL many, many stories. This truth was evident from the variety of compositions which evolved from art work, photography, color slides or other types of pictorial influences to which there was an exposure.

One of the year's favorite bulletin boards was one on which I would select a group of pictures which I had collected from the last *Miscellany* page of *Life* magazine. These would be mounted colorfully and given a number. The board heading would read *Pictures tell a Story*. After a day or so, when all the children had had a chance to investigate each unusual photograph closely, they were all bursting with ideas for a story. Usually one written story was not enough. Many children couldn't decide which picture they liked best so I might get two or three different stories from one student. The pictures came alive as the stories were read to the class. Then, with time permitting, we would have a story-telling period in which more interpretations of the pictures could be expressed.

These unusual photos were accepted with such enthusiasm that I repeated this technique for stimulating writing with a new group of pictures after a lapse of about three months. I was happy to see the same eagerness the second time round.

Picture selected: an arm holding up a golf club from the center of a pond of water.

A Great Day at Golf

This was the big day of the tournament. Mr Simon had, by one stroke, made it to the finals, and how he would love to win the trophy from that snobbish Mr Wilson. 'Boy, will that add some prestige to my position at the office,' he thought.

The competition was tough, and up to the last hole,

he was still in the running with a tying score of 77 to 77. Now came the real test, for the eighteenth hole was one of the toughest. Puddlewheel Pond was situated right in front of the green.

Mr Wilson made a straight drive, a good shot right down the fairway and landing on the edge of the green.

Now Mr Simon loosened up for his drive. One could tell that he was a little tense at this point. He moved up to the ball, took aim and . . . wham! The ball arched into the air and made a beautiful dive for the center of the pond.

'Ha!' said Mr Wilson. 'A lost ball will cost you a stroke, so I will win.'

'That is not a lost ball if I can hit from where it is, and that is just what I intend to do rather than lose this game to a big buffoon like you.' With that, Mr Simon jumped into the pool, searched around, and then all lost sight of him. In a few seconds out came a golf-ball flying from the pond and heading straight for the green. It rolled slowly, slowly and plop . . . right into the cup.

Mr Wilson rubbed his eyes, not wanting to believe what he had seen.

As Mr Simon came splashing out of the water the crowd cheered. The trophy was his and this was one match he would never forget.

*

On my schedule of field trips, the art museum is first on the list. I am surprised to see that most every year over half of my students have never been to an art museum. An exposure to good art is like an exposure to good books. It makes one aware of the many effective styles of communication available to man. I don't expect my students, necessarily, to become great artists or writers, but to be exposed to great works can provide an aesthetic enjoyment of our cultural heritage. Both good literature and good art can fulfil one's need for growth, security and beauty. To elevate the tastes of the young, I believe, is to ensure a better tomorrow.

Before our trip to the museum I have a bulletin board display of some of the paintings which would be seen at the

Phoenix Art Museum and on another board I display some of the great paintings of the world. We talk a little of the different styles of work and the periods in which they were painted. I suggest that the students be alert for some of these different styles during our trip and see which is more to their liking.

This seemed to be incentive enough on one visit, for I toured the museum with a group of serious spectators acting like connoisseurs looking for a masterpiece.

The next day the class bubbled with talk of what they had seen. After some release of the steam which could not be penned in any longer, we took pen in hand and wrote about the picture that was most impressive.

*

Great paintings also served us in another writing assignment and this was from a display of color prints. Before writing, there was a discussion of different forms of symbolism. How one might express love. What colors are more gay. Why one figure or object looks like a picture of strength whereas another appears weak and frail. I refrained from reading things into any one painting for I feel the enjoyment of a work of art is such a personal thing that one could curb another's insights by directing attentions to one's own interpretations.

I might point out the machine-like structure of Léger's figures and give a brief background of the Futuristic Movement, but not give a meaning for the picture. Or I might tell students to look closely at the colors of an impressionistic work so that they themselves could see how the eye makes the color green from the strokes of blue and yellow that were put on the canvas by the artist.

Then from a group of famous paintings children were told to write their own interpretations, being reminded that there was no one correct thought for the picture.

The Persistence of Memory by Salvador Dali

Limp, worn out clocks lying in a barren desert scene painted in Dali's surrealistic fashion:

> It means death. Everyone has so much time to use up and when that is gone there is nothing more.

(Written by a student who recently lost a grandmother and has been without a father since she was two years of age.)

The Starry Night by Vincent Van Gogh
Turbulent sky over a village scene:

> The world is filled with all types of problems, and no matter what people do in their own personal lives these problems are continually carried on. They may change somewhat throughout the ages but are always present.

Guernica by Pablo Picasso
Abstraction of figures with expressions of horror:

> Fear and hatred of war and death are shown in this painting. Yet people encourage slaughter with bullfights and new techniques of war equipment.

The Birthday by Marc Chagall
Kitchen scene of a man kissing a woman:

> The girl has swept the man off his feet with her loveliness and she is about to be flying herself since he remembered her birthday with a bouquet of flowers.

Titles of paintings were not given to students before the writings, so Debbie, who made this interpretation, was quite pleased when she learned the name of the painting and was also told of the love that Chagall had for his wife Beulah, who is supposedly represented in this work.

*

I have never ceased to be amazed at what children write. The insight and feelings which were expressed in the interpretations of paintings revealed understandings which seemed far beyond the experiences of eleven and twelve year olds. Such results made me want to strive harder for new situations in writing. I could see that I had before me a gold-mine of penned-in ideas and understandings. It was my responsibility to pull these riches out cautiously and gradually so as not to cause a cave-in of the vast potential present.

The elements of pictorial composition if properly directed

76

are usually freely expressed by children. One would not think of taking a brush and changing Johnny's painting or giving him a long set of rules to memorise before letting him try his hand at painting a picture. Yet for some reason there are those who feel that one should first learn the correct grammatical forms before attempting to do creative writing. Here again I would like to stress the importance I have found in letting students experiment, in giving them the freedom of self expression. The self-evaluation by seeing, sharing and reading is quite effective in making the writer aware of what constitutes good composition. Once these sensitivities are realised they are carried over into one's own work.

This does not go to say that children should not be given training in writing form or be lacking in the tools of language. These steps toward grammatical excellence must be gradual. First, the children must achieve some form of success so that they know they are capable of expressing worthwhile thoughts in their writing. As an artist learns to adjust various elements in his painting to make a better picture, so can the writer be taught to make corrections for better compositions. But these lessons are not taught by wielding a red pencil on a paper that took much effort by an individual.

*

I told each child to draw a head on a $12'' \times 18''$ piece of paper. Any type of head would do so long as it filled the whole piece of paper. It could be happy, sad, angry, frightened, odd or a self-portrait. From the results came comments which led to our story time:

'Tony's picture looks like a man from outer space.'

'No, it looks like a fellow who came from the grave.'

'I think it looks like Frankenstein's pal.'

What more is needed? With such interests aroused, Tony's picture became the character for our day's story.

Watch out for Walley

Walley Wicked was a devil of a fellow who could not stand good little boys. How disgusting it was to see Tommy mind his mother, do a good job with his schoolwork, or try to be a good boy scout.

'I must help Tommy be my kind of guy,' he thought.

That night, as Tommy was in bed, a strange feeling crept over him. He began thinking of how unfairly he had been treated all day. Why, if he had pretended to have forgotten about being home by four o'clock, he might have gotten out of mowing the lawn. Why should he have to mow the lawn each week? He didn't plant that crazy grass. And why had he been so foolish as to offer to help old widow Schultz next door? Just because she was eighty years old was no reason she couldn't carry out her own garbage cans. Maybe, Tommy thought, if I tell my teacher I lost my paper she'll excuse me from my arithmetic assignment. Heck, he didn't want to grow up to be a mathematician, so why should he have to bother with all those silly problems. Besides, when he grew up there would be machines capable of doing all the figuring.

Tommy seemed to have dozed off to sleep, but when he woke up the next morning he was so tired he felt as if he had been up all night.

'Breakfast,' called his mother.

'What are we having?' asked Tommy.

'Scrambled eggs on toast,' was the answer.

'You know I don't like my eggs scrambled and besides the toast looks too brown. I won't eat it.'

'Very well,' said his mother.

And off Tommy went to school making sure he slammed the door hard enough so everyone knew he had been treated unfairly.

On the school bus all the children had silly smiles on their faces as if they didn't know where that yellow monster of a bus was taking them. Tommy glared at all the stupid kids. As he stumbled off the bus he kicked a boy from behind then looked the other way as if he didn't know what had happened.

The bell rang much too soon and as Miss Thompson entered the room Tommy realised that he didn't have a pretty teacher after all. He must have been blind all those other days. Not only was she uglier than he had remembered, but she also gave harder assignments and was meaner.

The lunch in the cafeteria that day wasn't fit for pigs. After telling his class-mates that they must really be hard up to eat such slop, Tommy took his whole tray back to the kitchen untouched.

All the other boys cheated in the noon ball game by pitching him fast balls and calling him out when he was really safe.

He hated school!

After a miserable day, he returned home, stormed into the house, slammed his books on the table, kicked the cat, and then looked in the refrigerator to see if there was any chocolate milk left. Heck, his sister always got the last of the good things to eat, and with that he slammed the door so hard that he woke up his mother who was taking a nap.

'Good afternoon, dear, would you please run an errand for me?'

Why should everyone always be giving him things to do?

By supper time Tommy was so hungry that he didn't notice his mother had gone to the trouble of making his favorite dessert, banana cream pie. He just grunted a little as he ate his second piece.

Judy, his sister, politely asked if Tommy would help with the dishes since she had to work on a science project that evening.

'Not on your life. It's not my turn to do dishes and besides I'm going to watch TV,' and out of the room he scooted.

That evening, as Tommy put his head on the pillow, Walley Wicked smiled. My, what a successful day this had been.

*

The class did such clever work in making their Easter bonnets (see page 68) during an art assignment that I felt they were ready for costume designing. Near the end of the year, as a culminating exercise for our social studies units, I suggested that they divide into groups of three with one student acting as a model and the other two as designers. They were to create a costume appropriate to one of the periods of history or famous persons whom we had studied.

Before we could present our style show to another class we had to write descriptions for each outfit. These were read by one of the designers as the model 'gracefully' strolled across the room. What fun this turned out to be!

> Athena, goddess of Wisdom. Notice how she floats across the heavens. Speak, oh goddess!
> 'Oh dear, I'm so brilliant that all the men are after me. Why, even Herb Alpert of the Tijuana Brass is dying to marry me.'

Her costume was made from old white sheets which I usually have on hand for such things as paint cloths, togas and flags. She wore a curtain veil over her head with pearls for trimming.

> After the bullfights in Spain, you may like to go dancing with this charming señorita. The hand embroidery work kept this lady home many evenings preparing for this festive occasion.

Sharlene wore a fully decorated black skirt. One of the other students brought her a black lace scarf which was set on her head with high combs. She carried a red rose which she threw to the spectators.

> If you ever get a chance to see the Russian ballet in Moscow, you may see our darling ballerina.

This outfit stopped the show for a while. As Alan entered dancing and spinning in his strapless ballet outfit, the audience was in an uproar. What surprises for everyone! Especially since Alan was one student whose parents were concerned because he was quite shy in a group.

This freedom that he and other boys exhibited in such projects, I feel, was an indirect result of the freedom and security they developed from our writing programme.

*

A patterned design of block printed pink formations on white was shown to the students; they were told that the snow was covered with such a pattern one day and that they were to explain the circumstances. Their imaginations set to work on such ideas as:

> Oh, some pink atoms must have fallen during the night. Of course, it's always like that, but it usually falls down in a blob. It always happens that way on Skeleton's Reef up North by way of Antarctica.

> During the night after it snowed, a flying saucer landed in our back yard. Three men got out. Whenever they took a step they made a pink footprint.

> Last night, the Martians landed and went out to look around and when they took off, the pink fuel left marks like a pattern.

> When an airplane carrying pink food coloring landed on a cloud, the pilot checked to see if everything was all right. He left the door open. When the plane took off, it left the pink food coloring on the cloud, and when it snowed, the pink coloring fell to earth.

> And so you see, the snowmaker was tired of just making plain white snow. He decided it was time for him to start being more artistic. He thought that pop art looked pretty neat, so he grabbed a paint brush and some pink paint and . . . well, I guess you can pretty well guess what he did. He painted pink designs all over the snow and stepped back to admire his work.

> Last night was Christmas. Those round spots are where Mr Claus (roughly referred to as 'Santa') sat. You see, he has to rest every once in a while. The others were made by his crazy two-footed reindeer.

*

From a blue block printed design of circles, swirls and dots children explained how a sky could obtain such a pattern.

> The sky got that way when all the stars and planets exploded, sending pictures all over the universe.

I guess Athena must have been crying because she is the only one that cries blue and green tears.

One morning I woke up and the sky was all blurry with beautiful circles and designs. Just then I remembered, today was the Fourth of July and they were shooting off fireworks.

One day the sun's gravity pull brought all the planets close to earth. It also brought their moons and their atmospheres along with them. This made all the clouds disappear and created a strange new pattern in the skies.

When the Martians came through the clouds the friction of their saucer caused the molecules to take on such a pattern.

Boy, those outer-space men must be selling a lot of those crazy raised doughnuts and toy hurricanes.

My brother was messing around with his chemical set and when a pretty girl walked by the window he flipped and all the chemicals blew up. Thank goodness he was safe, but the garage where he was working . . . Oh, what a mess.

The next morning when he went to clean it up, it had all evaporated into the sky. The gases made the sky look like blue circles and green clovers.

*

Along with abstractions, a new use for vague, unrealistic, blurred color slides might be mentioned. In other words unsuccessful attempts at photography can be put to good use. By overlapping two such slides, a strange effect was achieved. From the unreal came clear perceptions, well-written by scheming, imaginative minds. A blurred slide of a Jackson Pollock painting was projected with a close-up view of a group of leaves.

On the planet of Orames every object changed color each hour of the day. This was caused by a strange type of molecule in the Orames atmosphere which would change the reflection of the sun's rays. Plants might be orange in the morning and green in the afternoon, or change from lavender to yellow.

The people never knew what color their hair, skin or nails would be during the different hours of the day. There was a terrible problem in trying to pick out the right color of clothing to wear to school.

A slide of a bubbling water fountain was overlapped with one of a mirrored mosaic structure.

Thousands of eyes peered out of the glass bottomed submarine. These were curious eyes, for they belonged to the persons who were to be the first inhabitants of an underwater civilisation. Their city was going to be self-sufficient, living only on the resources of the sea.

No wonder there were signs of anxiety in their stares. Were there really enough resources in the ocean to keep them all alive?

*

Educational films are another possibility opening the door for writing ideas. With the many excellent audiovisual films available, there is an inexhaustable source of pictorial aids to further a creative writing program.

Chapter Eight

THE UNFINISHED STORY

OUR CREATIVE WRITING experiences started me on an eager search for new stories, stories which I could tell the class for both amusement and stimulation. Even though students were great 'ad libbers' with our oral games and puppets, they still loved to listen to a fascinating tale.

From jokes and from my imagination, or with the help of other teachers, I soon collected quite a variety of stories which I could tell at the opportune time. These tales were rarely revealed in the same manner twice, since the acting out of the various expressions and the actions of the characters would often change. At first, stories were more to the point, but as time passed the task became easier and I found myself enjoying the elaboration of minor points. Like good leather, story telling seems to improve with use.

As my search for story plots heightened, I began keeping a card file which could be referred to in a free moment that permitted a story.

Often when there was a peak of interest I would stop the story and ask my listeners to finish the tale in their own way.

These unfinished tales became one of our most popular sources for extended writing. Because of the variety in subject matter children tried many different approaches. As months passed I could see that the earlier exercises were being helpful in improving the writings. The result was greater variety in words, better punctuation, and more complete paragraph structure. Even though their papers were never red-penciled for grammatical errors, students were becoming more conscious in applying their language skills to their works, for they were now becoming more self-confident. They began to polish, refine, distil and look back at their work with a pleased eye. They were justly proud of the original arrangements in which they had expressed themselves. With so much writing going on one might have expected duplication but instead there was expansion and growth.

During a period of study on Egypt and its marvels of ancient pyramids and Pharaohs, I told a tale of Curious Kent.

A Vacation Away from Home

One day Curious Kent was walking down the narrow streets of Giza in Egypt. His curiosity was not amusing to two hooded Arabs who suspiciously chased him through the streets and finally into the desert.

Kent had never ridden a camel before and the one he purchased for his get-away was as awkward as any animal could be. As he turned to look for the men in pursuit of him, he was thrown to the ground. When he looked up he saw that he was in front of a huge pyramid. He began climbing and as he walked across one stone a huge slab wall rotated around, making a doorway.

Since he saw the men coming closer, he had no choice but to enter, and as he did the slab wall rotated back into place.

Here he is alone (so he thinks) inside an ancient Egyptian pyramid.

Kent looked around in the blackness and then thought of the matches he had in his pocket. When he had a little light he could see that he was in a narrow passageway. He felt his way down through the darkness until he came to a corner. He turned the corner and *plop!* He fell through a trap-door.

When his head was clear from the sudden shock of the fall he lit a match and saw that he was in what must have been a Pharaoh's chamber. There were beautiful carvings, solid gold statues and highly decorated furniture. He luckily saw an old torch and lit it.

Just as he was about to examine the treasures he heard noises so he wrapped a bolt of linen around him and quickly jumped into one of the mummy-cases.

It was kind of crowded with an old Egyptian friend laid out cold and stiff beside him, but he didn't have time to worry about that.

He lay there quietly and listened. The men entered the chamber and were talking in Arabic. Kent could tell that these were the same men who he had surprised in Giza.

One of them suddenly lifted the top of the mummy-case. Kent, having an itch, wiggled. The man shouted in fright. Kent realised then that this guy was really not as tough as he looked, so he slowly began to sit up. This was too much of a shock for the Arab. He fainted dead away.

The other fellow was not as chicken. He ran towards Kent with an ancient spear, but as Kent jumped out of the mummy-case, the spear landed in the other mummy.

Kent grabbed an old metal box and hit the second man over the head. There they were, both asleep side by side. Wrapping up his two mystery guests with the linen he had taken off himself, Kent found a paper. He discovered that this paper was an ancient map of the pyramid and must have been what the men were studying when he first surprised them in Giza.

Because of the map he had no trouble finding his way out of the pyramid. He hailed a passing camel and headed for the Egyptian State Patrol. They were not only pleased to have the two notorious robbers in captivity, but were extra pleased with the discovery of the ancient treasure. For this Kent was given a $5000 reward.

With this money Kent decided to take a restful vacation, so he booked passage for the Bahamas. While sitting on a deserted beach and appreciating the quiet sound of the surf he saw something washed ashore. He went over to take a closer look, for he thought his eyes were playing tricks with him. Before Curious Kent was a beautiful mermaid. She smiled and . . .

*

Another story, prompted by one of Dr Gattegno's, with enough of reality and a twist of the fantastic, aroused many different responses.

Rick, Rob and Rover

Rick and Rob, in an attempt to catch a strange animal which had left footprints on the ground, tied a small, almost invisible wire between two trees. When they whistle, their dog Rover gets caught in their trap and his head is cut off. But while it is still in the air, Rover realises what has happened and, in trying to catch his head, runs a little too far and the head lands on his tail.

What are the two boys to do with their dog whose head shakes every time his tail wags?

When the boys got home with Rover, Mother was quite shocked. She had no solutions to the problem and suggested the boys wait until Dad got home.

'In the meantime', she said, 'let's treat Rover to one of the steaks I have thawing for dinner.'

Well, Rover, who always got regular dog food, had never been treated so royally. When he saw the big juicy steak before him, his tail wagged so furiously that his head flipped off.

This time Rover was a little better on the timing and caught the head right on the stub of his neck. He smiled as dogs smile (with their wagging tails) and began eating his steak.

*

Valentine's Day seemed to bring on a new outlook, especially when investigated by a Hallowe'en witch.

The Wandering Wondering Witch

Henrietta Hobblywho slept in a cave with all the other witches until Hallowe'en when they all had their fun frightening people.

For some strange reason Henrietta was restless and couldn't sleep. Never before had she felt this way. She glanced at the calendar. Only February 14th so it was certainly too early to get up, but after three drinks of witches sleeping brew she was more awake then ever.

She decided that she would go for a ride on her broom before trying to get her sleep. What strange sights she saw on her ride! No monsters, no trick-or-treaters going from house to house, no ghosts out. Instead she saw people being friendly and nice to one another.

'Think I'll take a better look at these odd happenings,' said the witch.

As she peered into one house, she saw a husband and wife eating dinner. Suddenly the man pulled a large envelope from his pocket and handed it to the women. At this instant a strange little creature with a bow and arrow shot both the man and woman, and they just sat there smiling at one another.

'My, what strange people.'

Henrietta then saw a young boy prancing down the street with a box of candy. 'Think I'll follow him since he is probably going to trick someone,' thought the witch.

The boy walked up to a small white house. He knocked on the door. He put the box on the doorstep and ran away.

A pretty young girl came to the door and smiled as she leaned over to pick up the heart-shaped box.

'Why, he didn't even soap the windows and gave a treat instead of asking for one. My, what is this world coming to?'

Henrietta was so confused that she thought she was dreaming. She hurried back to the cave and set the alarm for October 31st. And you can be sure that she never did tell her witch friends about her adventures, for if she did they would surely think she was a wacky witch.

*

With the April winds come our story of flying kites.

Spring Spirit

Jerry had saved his allowance for a new kite. He wanted the best, so it had taken him a number of weeks to save for a beautiful red plastic streamlined model with the strongest string possible.

Having such a good kite made it less of a chore to fly. In no time at all Jerry was proudly demonstrating his skills with the complete 1200 feet of string extended from his prized possession, while the other boys looked on.

Just then he heard his mother call him. Not wanting to reel in the kite, he decided to tie it to a tree rather than leave it with the neighborhood bullies. That was before he saw Ricky, the smallest boy in school, who weighed no more than half of a watermelon.

'Ricky, how would you like to hold my kite?' yelled Jerry.

'Oh, boy, could I?' answered Ricky eagerly.

So he handed the kite to the beaming boy and turned to head for home as a big gust of wind came up and . . .

. . . before anyone could grab Ricky he was swept off his feet and was flying in the air.

Jerry looked back in horror. There went his allowance, and worse still was the fact that Ricky was going up higher and higher and getting smaller and smaller. He felt tears trickling down his face. Why was this happening and what could be done to save Ricky?

Before any bright idea struck him he saw something headed for his kite. Yes, it looked like a pair of wild ducks. These ducks were probably busy looking at the scenery below them because they didn't see the beautiful red dragon kite. They ran right into it, got tangled in the string, and came crashing to the ground right at Jerry's feet. Ricky came floating down behind them and strangely enough landed on a pile of hay that was in a nearby field.

Jerry looked at the two dead ducks in front of him. They had ruined his kite, but they were beautiful. He knew Mr Hooper, the taxidermist, would pay him enough to buy two kites and that is what he did.

He bought a yellow kite for Ricky and another red one for himself. The next day the two boys were out as before, flying their kites. But this time, just for insurance, Ricky was tied to a tree.

*

One evening I heard a joke about a parrot that couldn't

figure out how the magician had made a ship disappear when it was unexpectedly torpedoed. With these same characters a new story was developed for our writing.

Merlin's Magic

Merlin, the magician, offers to take good care of his friend's pet parrot while the friend is on vacation. This is fine and helpful to Merlin in the beginning since the parrot is used as an assistant in his magic act. But once the wise bird learns the tricks he can't keep his mouth shut and informs the audiences of what is happening. Consequently the crowds start dwindling and Merlin realises that he must do something before he is ruined.

He finally decides on some new magic which will not only solve his problem but will still allow him to keep his promise to his friend.

Merlin bought six beautiful silk scarfs for his new act. During the performance he said, 'Now ladies and gentlemen, with my assistant, Pepe, the parrot, I will do my newest bit of magic.'

Pepe eagerly flew to his perch near Merlin. Merlin showed the red scarf to the audience and then tied it around Pepe's crooked beak. He then held up the pure yellow scarf. After the audience got a good look at it, he tied it to the red scarf. Then he added a green scarf, a purple scarf, a blue one, and last of all a white scarf with black dots. These colorful scarfs hung from Pepe's beak to the floor. Merlin then took all the scarfs and wound them around the beak like a big bandage which ended up to be larger than Pepe's head. He then told Pepe to fly around the stage while he said the magic words.

When Pepe was called back to his perch, Merlin carefully unwound the bandage so the audience could see that there was now one huge scarf with beautiful mixed colours of red, green, yellow, blue, purple and white with black dots spattered through the design. The end of the large scarf was tied to Pepe's beak just as the first red scarf had been.

There was a great applause of approval from the audience. Pepe could see that everyone liked this act so there was no complaining when Merlin left the huge scarf tied around his beak until the show was over. In this there was no chance for Pepe to chatter away. And so the great magician and the parrot continued in their partnership until the happy day when the owner came back to get his pet.

*

I decided to try to reverse the process by reading the last paragraph of a story to the class and asking them to fill in the part that came before.

. . . and seeing the pleased looks on his mother's and dad's faces, Kim realised that never again would he be treated like a baby, for he had now proven that he could be a responsible person.

The Campout

'Ah, stop crying,' said Kim disgustedly to Alfred. 'We'll find the camp soon.'

'But we've been looking all afternoon and it's starting to get dark.'

'If we had carried our compasses like Mr Cooper told us to, we would know in what direction to head, and with it being cloudy all day the sun can't even help us. If we don't find the other boys in another hour we had better find a place to make ourselves comfortable.'

Kim had always been a pretty good boy scout. Guess that is why Mr Cooper had asked him to have Alfred as his partner during this trip. This was spoiled Alfred's first campout and he was such a sissy.

Alfred didn't argue with Kim's suggestion, but anyone could tell by the look on his face that he was frightened and didn't trust his partner's judgment completely.

'Let's collect enough twigs for a fire and a covering for our beds. It will be getting cold tonight and we don't have too much clothing with us,' said Kim.

Rubbing sticks together for a spark didn't seem as easy as it was during the camp skill test, but finally Kim had a nice fire going, just at a time when the boys needed the extra heat.

With pangs of hunger in their stomachs, neither of the boys was sleepy. No wild berries or nuts around like in the fairy tales. Kim did have a stick of gum in his pocket that he shared with Alfred.

This was not a night for ghost stories since they were both frightened enough, so Kim talked to Alfred about his plans for the summer until he was too sleepy to listen and dropped off to sleep.

It was a restless night with the cold biting air, the hard ground, and the worry of wild animals. Dawn finally did come and the boys gave each other somewhat of a smile as they opened their eyes.

'Today we are not going to move around,' said Kim. 'Mr Cooper will realise we are lost and send someone out looking for us. Today we will set up camp in that clearing over there and see if we can make any type of signal to alert a rescue party.'

By the third day even Kim was getting a little worried, but he tried not to show his fear to Alfred, who by this time was like a two year old.

The gum was getting kind of rubbery, but it felt good having something in their mouths since all they had eaten were a couple of roots from some plants.

Kim looked at Alfred as he lay under the tree. 'He has enough reserve fat in him to last a week,' he thought to himself. 'Oh dear, on second thoughts, I hope it won't be that long before we are found.'

Just then he heard a noise in the distance. He yelled and yelled, then listened. Sure enough, someone was coming. With the voices nearer, Kim was able to direct the group to the clearing. Oh, how happy the boys were!

The three men who were part of a twenty-member rescue party carried the boys back to camp. There Alfred and Kim were met by their parents.

Alfred, who had been crying for most of the three

days, now began talking like a magpie. He told the group how Kim had remembered all his scout training and kept calm. Alfred was now sounding like he himself had grown up.

Kim looked at his parents, and seeing the pleased looks on his mother's and dad's faces, Kim realised that never again would he be treated like a baby, for he had now proven that he could be a responsible person.

Chapter Nine

IN SUMMARY

FROM THE TOYING and explorations of working with words, their relationships and combinations, we came to realise that we had only touched the surface of the numerous possibilities in which they could be arranged to express reality. Never could the possibilities be exhausted for in each child was a volcano ready to erupt at the right moment of stimulation.

One of the original goals in this writing project was to see a greater freedom of expression being released from the writings of children. Accepting a child at his own level of achievement developed a better understanding of each individual.

To disregard grades for creative efforts seemed to be a great step in opening the door to original thinking. Of course, spelling, punctuation and grammatical skills were not thrown aside. These were considered elsewhere in the teaching schedule. Children relaxed under this freedom and soon learned to tell, write, and express ideas with greater ease.

This non-evaluating role is very difficult for teachers since it is contrary to all their training and tradition. We have been taught to judge things good or bad, mark things right or wrong, give a work a plus or minus. But there is not right or wrong when it comes to creativity. Who is qualified to judge when it comes to grading a child's creative effort? The job of the teacher is to set the stage, then stand back and not interfere with the productive outpourings of the individuals.

From this new freedom there was a satisfaction in the creation of original works. Students dared to be different. Having gained self-respect and confidence they were not afraid to try new approaches to a problem. Not always were the results successful, but, aided by group activities which acted as a stimulus as well as a testing audience, creative powers were improved and nurtured.

94

Then during a period of aloneness came the real creations. With personal experiences and sensitivities drawn on, an internal combustion seemed to be released on paper.

The recognition of the importance of individuality in writing was felt throughout our exercises. We did not withhold appreciation when a new spark of thought excited the group.

Since students were not penalised for misspelled words, their writing vocabulary approached their speaking vocabulary. With a continual challenge of uniqueness there was also a search for new words. This automatically increased vocabulary ranges in our writers. Along with our interest in good books there developed an appreciation of the power and potential of verbal expression.

With a lack of rigidity in the classroom students learned to toy with the elements of language. They developed skills in juggling elements so that evolutionary forms of written communication resulted.

There were those times when problems were hard to master, but these conflicts, rather than becoming a cause for frustrations, brought about a sense of wondering. Conflicts developed both strength and character as children learned to experience them and face them intellectually.

The pleasure derived from the satisfaction of the children's work increased my enthusiasm. This in itself was something that the class detected and from it we all benefited. Children have a way of seeing enthusiasm, and mine could not be hidden as words were dispensed and generated into thousands of colorful ideas.

The real satisfaction in this approach comes from watching the children's growth during the creative process. The hours of compiling and selecting the writings for this book were most worthwhile if they arouse a curiosity in the reader to try setting a new stage for new groups. In this way more and more children will become imbued with the joys of releasing their creative potential through writing.